The Easy Allergy-Free Cookbook

THE EASY Allergy-Free Cookbook

85 Recipes **without** Gluten, Dairy, Tree Nuts, Peanuts, Eggs, Fish, Shellfish, Soy, or Wheat

AMANDA ORLANDO

ROCKRIDGE
PRESS

Interior and Cover Designer: Scott Wooledge
Art Producer: Janice Ackerman
Editor: Owen Holmes
Production Editor: Jax Berman
Production Manager: Holly Haydash

Photography: ©Nadine Greeff: pp. vi, 100, 125; ©Evi Abeler: pp. xii, 53, 91; Shutterstock: pp. 10–12; ©Andrew Purcell: pp. 16, 30, 57; ©Hélène Dujardin: pp. 21, 48, 66, 82, 114; ©Darren Muir: p. 35; ©Leigh Beisch: p. 111

Illustration: Courtesy of The Noun Project

Paperback ISBN: 978-1-63878-200-1 | eBook ISBN: 978-1-63878-580-4
R0

This book is dedicated
to my family.

Flank Steak with
Chimichurri, page 93

Contents

Introduction

Welcome to the *Easy Allergy-Free Cookbook*. I'm Amanda Orlando, an adult living with multiple anaphylactic food allergies. I'm also the blogger behind @EverydayAllergenFree, where I share crave-worthy, free-from recipes and my journey through life with allergies.

I was diagnosed with allergies and eczema at just a few months old. Although I outgrew some of my allergies, most of them have stuck around for the long haul. A couple of new ones even developed as I got older, but there's no way that's stopping me from enjoying delicious food. I can say (without hyperbole) that food is the one topic I think about most in life: Where can I get this exciting new ingredient? When can I try out that technique I saw online? And most important, what am I making for dinner?

Receiving a diagnosis for yourself or a loved one can feel heavy and stressful. Perhaps the foods and rituals you enjoyed most have been greatly impacted, or maybe you are having difficulty structuring meals without former key ingredients in your home. While living with food allergies is an ongoing and ever-changing journey, you will always find a way to make things work. There are so many incredible foods out there, so you may just require a shift of focus and perspective. After being diagnosed with an allergy, packaged foods in particular often become a sudden obstacle. They are no longer the convenience they once were. As you get into the groove of reading every label, every time, you will quickly notice that many of the top food allergens are found in a great many packaged foods, whether in their whole form or as additives. You may find yourself questioning what "may contain" statements mean and whether you should call a food manufacturer to determine if allergenic products were produced on the same lines as something that would otherwise be safe for you. You may not be able to rely on certain packaged foods anymore.

The biggest piece of advice I can offer here is to focus on fresh whole food ingredients, as well as the multitude of allergy-safe foods you can create from them. When you do that, you know exactly what you're eating and you're in control.

With the 85 carefully selected recipes in this book, you will be well equipped to cook any meal quickly and easily. And your meals will not skimp on flavor! At times it can feel like avoiding common allergens, such as dairy or soy, strips the flavor from your meals. However, once you reframe your idea of what meal components are to focus on other flavorings, such as herbs and spices, you'll see that there is no compromise on deliciousness.

In chapter 1, we walk through some tips for making your home allergy safe so that you can cook allergy-free with ease. You'll learn about the difference between a dish being "clean" versus it being "allergy clean," avoiding cross contamination, stocking an allergy-free kitchen, some practical ways to communicate about your allergies with others in your home, and more. Chapters 2 through 8 provide easy recipes (from breakfast to dessert) made using accessible and common whole food ingredients. They even include vegetarian and vegan recipes, as well as meat-forward recipes, so that you can find meals that suit your preferences. The last chapter includes basic staples that you can use again and again in your kitchen, making it easier to live without those packaged goods. The best part? The majority of the recipes are ready within 30 minutes, which is ideal for weekday meals.

While this book aims to be as inclusive as possible, it does not address every dietary restriction or option, so please consult with your allergist or doctor for additional dietary information.

Cooking allergy-friendly food is an exciting and constantly evolving journey. Be patient with yourself and take a moment to appreciate that this way of cooking might be flipping everything that you used to know about mealtimes on its head. Know that you are capable of creating incredibly delicious and satisfying food. Let's get cooking.

Chicken and Carrot
Pan Bake, page 69

CHAPTER 1

Easy Allergy-Free Cooking

COOKING ALLERGY-FREE MEALS CAN BE SIMPLE, easy, and delicious. This chapter explores how you can set yourself (and your kitchen) up for success and make mealtime easier. You'll discover helpful resources that outline the tasty foods that you can use liberally in your cooking, as well as those you should avoid (and their substitutes).

Making Allergy-Free Cooking Easy

If you're new to the world of allergy-free cooking, you might be thinking, "But what about all of the scratch cooking, preplanning, and specialty ingredients?" It can seem like a hassle to find inexpensive allergy-free ingredients and time consuming to cook from scratch, but this book will guide you through a simpler and more pared-down approach.

My approach is to use basic, accessible, and familiar ingredients to create fabulous meals that you will enjoy. The recipes are well suited for any beginner cook or baker, because they require little prep or cleanup time and most can be made in 30 minutes or less. Additionally, most of the recipes call for five ingredients or fewer (excluding salt, pepper, and oil), many of which you will likely already have on hand. Many recipes are one-pot, meaning less mess and cleanup, less clanging around in the kitchen, and more time to enjoy your delicious homemade meals. I want you to flip through this book and think, "I can do all of this!"

Creating Your Allergy-Free Kitchen

The recipes in this book are free from the eight most common food allergens: peanuts, tree nuts, dairy, eggs, soy, wheat, fish, and shellfish. They are also suitable for those with gluten or dairy intolerances. Often, we are cooking for multiple allergies, which can be a challenge. However, this book provides plenty of great recipes and ingredient ideas so that weekly meal planning won't feel like a chore or a sacrifice.

Whether you are cooking for yourself or for a family member who has food allergies, you will find this book is a helpful source of recipe ideas and a springboard for inspiration. Still, allergy-free cooking requires good judgment and a certain level of care. Here are some things to keep in mind as you build your allergy-free kitchen.

Avoid cross contamination: An allergy-safe food can come into contact with a potential allergen through seemingly innocuous actions, such as using the same knife, utensils, or cutting board or not washing your hands after touching an allergen. Even the smallest amount of an allergen can cause an anaphylactic reaction in individuals with food allergies. Just because you cannot see the allergen (e.g., there are no visible crumbs) does not mean that particles do not remain on a surface. To avoid cross contamination, wash your hands, utensils, cutting boards, and any other surfaces thoroughly with a clean sponge and hot, soapy water before preparing an allergy-safe dish. Note that hand sanitizer does not remove

---

TIME-SAVING TIPS

Here are a few suggestions for saving time in the kitchen:

→ Cook a double batch and freeze the extra portions for meals in a pinch.

→ Wash, stem, peel, and freeze berries and bananas together for "nice cream" at the ready.

→ Do all of your washing and chopping for the week in one sitting to reduce prep time later on.

→ Write down your meal plan on Sunday to make shopping easier.

→ Each week, choose recipes that use the same ingredients to minimize wasting produce and money.

allergens. It's a good idea to keep allergen equipment and allergy-free equipment completely separate. For example, you may have containers reserved only for storing allergy-free food. You may have a separate cutting board for allergy-free food. Finally, never store ingredients in containers that once held allergens, such as storing tea in an old peanut butter jar.

Keep your kitchen stocked with safe ingredients: Read every ingredient label, every time, to ensure it is allergy safe. Once you know an ingredient is allergy-free, keep your pantry stocked so you'll always have what you need on hand. We'll discuss this more in the following pages.

Be prepared: Keep your EpiPen handy in kitchen and dining spaces. Print an allergen list and post it on the refrigerator, or another easily accessible place, and include the allergens' pseudonyms and foods they are commonly found in.

Use good judgment: When adjusting your kitchen to be allergy-free, use good judgment for assessing potential cross contamination. When in doubt, wash (your hands, pots, pans, etc.) again. If you think a pantry staple may have been contaminated in the past (e.g., flour contaminated by a buttery measuring cup while baking), do not use it.

ALLERGY-FREE SHOPPING TIPS

Here are four of my favorite tips for less-stressful allergy-free shopping.

→ Read the ingredient label more than once, even if the product seems like one pure ingredient. Scan the package for "contains" or "may contain" statements, as well as allergen control protocol statements. Depending on your country and region, "may contain" statements may be voluntary and allergen information may be displayed differently.

→ Don't buy a new product if you are not sure about its ingredients. Take a quick picture of the product, then research it at home. If you feel it is necessary, you can contact the manufacturer for more information. If you decide it's the right fit, then purchase it later.

→ Shop the fresh produce and protein aisles first. By the time you get to the packaged or frozen food aisles, you may be pleasantly surprised by the abundance already in your cart.

Foods to Enjoy

Let's explore some of the delicious foods that you can enjoy even if you have any combination of the top eight allergies.

Fruits and Vegetables

Eating a balanced diet with full daily servings of fruits and vegetables is especially important if your diet is already limited due to allergies or intolerances. Fruits and vegetables help provide essential nutrients that may be missed when avoiding allergens.

Apples: There are thousands of varieties, and each variety has a unique flavor and texture.

Citrus fruits: Liven up soups, salad dressings, and breakfast plates with colorful citrus fruits.

Dark leafy greens: For variety in flavor, try different greens, such as Swiss chard, rapini, or dinosaur kale.

Root vegetables: Roast, bake, sauté, or steam root vegetables such as sweet potatoes or bitter parsnips for a delicious, starchy side.

Meat

Meats are not among the top eight allergens, so take the opportunity to explore this category of foods. However, you may need to limit meat in your diet for other health reasons. The newest FDA Dietary Guidelines recommend 23 to 33 ounces of meat-based protein foods per week, with the rest of the protein requirements coming from other sources, such as legumes, seeds, and beans.

Beef: Beef is a great source of protein, iron, and zinc. Health professionals often recommend small portions of beef due to associated health risks, so you may consider saving beef for special occasions.

Chicken: Chicken can be used in so many ways, such as roasting the whole bird or making stock. Chicken is a low-fat source of protein. Cook a batch, shred or dice it, and then freeze it to add to meals later.

Lamb: Lamb is rich in vitamins and minerals and includes all nine essential amino acids. It's incredible on the barbeque or slow roasted in the oven with garlic and rosemary.

Pork: Pork is another high-quality source of protein and is super versatile. Sear pork chops, make a pork loin, or use ground pork in meat loaf and meatballs.

Turkey: This poultry is not just for Thanksgiving. Purchase trimmed turkey breasts to use instead of chicken in soups, stews, and roast dinners.

Legumes and Seeds

Legumes and seeds are excellent sources of fiber and plant-based protein, especially when you can't eat tree nuts and soy.

Flaxseed and chia seeds: Sprinkle these on salads and cereal or mix with water to create an egg replacer in baking recipes.

Lentils: Lentils are a part of the legume family and come in several varieties. You can find them canned, but many dried varieties cook quickly and are great additions to soups, salads, and side dishes.

Red, white, and black beans: Beans are super versatile. Add them to soups, blend for dips and sauces, or toss into salads. Canned varieties are convenient, but dried varieties have a longer shelf life.

Shelled sunflower and pumpkin seeds: These add the perfect crunch to baked goods, salads, and snacks.

Spices and Herbs

Luckily, most spices and herbs don't contain allergens, and they bring tons of flavor to dishes. Try both fresh and dried varieties. Here are some of my go-to spices and herbs.

Dried oregano: Add a flavorful punch to salad dressings and meat marinades.

Dried paprika: Sprinkle it on potatoes, use it as a rub for beef, or add it to chili for beautiful color and a light barbecue flavor.

Fresh basil: Peppery and aromatic, this herb can be added to tomato sauce, salads, grilled vegetables, and marinades.

Fresh cilantro: For a pop of fresh flavor and color, sprinkle it on stir-fried meat or vegetables, soups, and stews.

Fresh or dried ground ginger: A dynamic and flexible spice, ginger can be used fresh or dried in both sweet and savory dishes.

Ground cinnamon: Spice up your baking with the aroma of ground cinnamon.

Quinoa and Rice

Gluten-free grains open a world of possibilities because they can be eaten in their whole form or made into flours and dairy-free milks. They are nutrient dense; some are complete proteins on their own, and others are made complete proteins with the addition of legumes.

Brown rice flour: This is commonly used as the base flour in many gluten-free 1-to-1 flour mixes due to its pleasant taste and texture.

Rice: Try all types of rice, including white, brown, short grain, and long grain. Rice milk can be made from white or brown varieties of rice and often comes enriched with added nutrients.

Tapioca starch: The starch of the tapioca root is an amazing binding and thickening agent in gravy, sauces, soups, and baking.

White or red quinoa: Filling and flavorful, this grain cooks in about 15 minutes and is a complete protein, too.

Foods to Avoid and Substitute

While you may not be allergic to all eight of the top allergens (or you may have allergies outside the top eight), the following foods represent the most common allergens that people with multiple food allergies avoid. In this section you will also find substitutes for all eight allergens. This list does not include every allergen pseudonym, but it will get the ball rolling on your allergen research.

Milk

This category includes any product derived from dairy (cow's milk, goat's milk, etc.) and lab-grown dairy proteins (a new plant-based development). Common examples include butter, ghee, milk, cream, yogurt, cheese, sour cream, ice cream, and additives such as lactose, casein, stearic acid, and whey. Milk derivatives are often found in frozen foods, snacks, chips, crackers, deli meats, packaged bread crumbs, cereals, pastries, canned or frozen soups, breads, and more.

Alternatives include dairy-free milks, such as rice milk or sunflower milk. These can be used on morning cereal, in baking, or even in savory recipes if they are not sweetened or flavored. Olive oil can be used to replace butter in nearly every savory recipe. Nutritional yeast can offer a similar taste to Parmesan cheese in pastas and other dishes.

Egg

This category includes eggs from any poultry (chicken, duck, quail, etc.). On labels, it may be called albumin, lecithin, or an array of additives beginning with the "ovo-" prefix. Eggs are commonly found in baked goods (inside or as a glaze), ice cream, mayonnaise, salad dressings, eggnog, meringue, desserts, mixed alcoholic drinks, pasta, burger patties and meatballs, and more.

You can try a commercial egg substitute or you can mix 1 tablespoon of chia seeds or flaxseed (whole or ground) with 2 tablespoons of water to create a homemade egg substitute. Just wait a few minutes for the mixture to thicken. Egg can also be replaced with ⅓ cup of unsweetened applesauce or mashed banana in baking recipes or 1 tablespoon of apple cider vinegar or white vinegar as a leavening agent.

Shellfish

A very broad category, shellfish can include crustaceans, mollusks, cephalopods, bivalves, and gastropods. How shellfish is labeled as an allergen can differ by country or region. Examples include shrimp or prawns, lobster, crab, scallops, snails, mussels, clams, squid, cuttlefish, scampi, crawfish, oysters, and octopus. They can be found in ceviche, sauces, stews, soups, and pastas, as well as dried, grilled, steamed, fried, or simply raw.

In stews or pasta dishes that call for shellfish, try using chicken or sliced king oyster mushrooms instead.

Fish

This includes any type or size of swimming fish, with meat of any variety (white, oily, pink, etc.). Some popular examples include salmon, trout, perch, bass, tuna (also referred to as yellowfin or albacore), sardines, anchovies, cod, haddock, sole, tilapia, and catfish. Fish is commonly found in stews and soups or fried, grilled, tinned, salted, packed in oil or water, or fermented. Anchovies are commonly found in Worcestershire sauce, many barbecue sauces, fish sauce and stock, Caesar dressing, olive tapenade, dips, and some pasta sauces such as puttanesca.

Make your own Barbecue Sauce (page 123), tapenade, and dressings at home. Anchovies are often used in these foods because they have an umami (savory) flavor, which you can replace with balsamic vinegar or capers in many recipes.

Wheat

Wheat refers to the grain, not just the gluten protein. Wheat is found in spelt, farro (an ancient variety of wheat that resembles puffy brown rice), wheat berries, bulgur, farina, semolina flour, durum flour, seitan (pure wheat gluten), modified food starch, einkorn, malt, kamut, and MSG (monosodium glutamate). Wheat or gluten ingredients can be found in dressings, mustards, sauces, oats (due to cross contamination during processing), baked goods, burgers and meatballs, pastries, pasta, soy sauce, matzo meal, cereal, couscous, and more.

Allergy-free 1-to-1 flour mixes are great for baking, especially if you are not comfortable mixing your own flour mix or do not have time. Rice noodles and pastas made from corn or quinoa are excellent alternatives to wheat pasta. Instead of MSG, add more salt as desired. Gluten-free bread crumbs and certified gluten-free oats can be used to bind burgers and meatballs. Use quinoa where you would normally use couscous.

Soy

This refers to any product derived from soybeans, such as edamame (whole soybeans), tofu, soy sauce, soy oil, soya, soy lecithin, miso, soy protein, hydrolyzed soy protein, soy flour, soy milk, natto, and tempeh. You would be surprised by how many packaged foods contain soy. It can seem like soy is everywhere. Watch out for soy as an additive in bottled sauces and dressings, shortening, fried foods, frozen foods, plant-based protein powders, plant-based milks, plant-based ice creams, breads, margarine, vegan butters, vegan cheeses, and many other packaged foods (both sweet and savory).

Canola, sunflower, or avocado oil can be used as an alternative to soy oil. Rice milk can be used in place of soy milk. Lard can be used instead of shortening or vegan butters in a 1:1 ratio. Hemp protein powder is a great substitute for soy-based protein powders. Shredded seaweed or balsamic vinegar can add a deep umami flavor when replacing soy sauce in a stir-fry.

Tree Nuts

This category refers to a long list of tree nut varieties, such as Brazil nuts, hazelnuts, chestnuts, almonds, pistachios, walnuts, cashews, macadamia nuts, and pine nuts. Coconut is considered a tree nut in some countries, such as the United States, but not others, such as Canada. Tree nuts are commonly found fresh or dried; shelled or unshelled; added into other food items, such as sauces, marinades, chocolate, cereals, baked goods, salads, soups, and stews; and processed into flours, butters, oils, milks, and cheeses.

Seeds are an easy alternative to tree nuts and still offer a wide variety of sizes, textures, and tastes. You can also buy seed oils that have a nutty profile, such as flaxseed oil. Legumes may also be a good option, depending on the recipe. If seeking a quick protein for a salad, try adding canned whole black beans or kidney beans.

Peanuts

This legume can be found in its whole form; processed into peanut butter, peanut oil, and peanut milk; chopped and sprinkled on top of hot dishes or salads; ground into flour; and used in bottled sauces, dressings, and desserts, such as pastries, cookies, candies, chocolate, taffy, ice cream, and other frozen treats.

Foods to Avoid and Their Substitutes

 MILK

FOODS TO AVOID Any product derived from dairy (cow's milk, goat's milk, etc.) or lab-grown dairy proteins (such as butter, ghee, milk, cream, yogurt, cheese, sour cream, and ice cream), and additives such as lactose, casein, stearic acid, and whey

UNEXPECTED SOURCES frozen foods, snacks, chips, crackers, deli meats, packaged bread crumbs, cereals, pastries, canned or frozen soups, custards, breads, frozen treats, desserts, chocolate, pesto

SUBSTITUTES TO TRY Oat milk, rice milk, quinoa milk, hemp milk, sunflower milk, nondairy yogurt made from oat milk, lard, olive oil, and nutritional yeast

 EGGS

FOODS TO AVOID Egg from any poultry (chicken, duck, quail, etc.), albumin, lecithin, and additives beginning with the prefix "ovo-"

UNEXPECTED SOURCES hollandaise sauce, mayonnaise, salad dressings, eggnog, desserts (such as meringue, chocolate mousse, custard, baked goods, and ice cream), mixed drinks such as whiskey sour and pisco sour, carpaccio, pasta (noodles and preparations such as carbonara), breads, burger patties, meatballs, and glazes on breads

SUBSTITUTES TO TRY Flax egg (1 tablespoon of flaxseed or chai seeds mixed with 2 tablespoons of water and set aside to thicken), ⅓ cup unsweetened applesauce or mashed banana per egg in baking recipes, and 1 tablespoon of white or apple cider vinegar as a leavening agent

 SHELLFISH

FOODS TO AVOID Shrimp, prawns, lobster, crab, scallops, snails, mussels, clams, squid, cuttlefish, scampi, crawfish, oysters, octopus, shrimp sauce, dried shrimp, dried cod, fish stock, and seafood stock

UNEXPECTED SOURCES stews and soups, pastas, fish sauces by other names (such as nam prik and mam tom), and imitation shellfish

SUBSTITUTES TO TRY Chicken and sliced king oyster mushrooms

 # FISH

FOODS TO AVOID All fish (including salmon, trout, perch, bass, yellowfin and albacore tuna, sardines, anchovies, cod, haddock, sole, tilapia, and catfish), fish oil, fish sauce, and fish stock

UNEXPECTED SOURCES stews and soups, Worcestershire sauce, barbecue sauce, Caesar dressing, olive tapenade and other dips, and pasta sauces such as puttanesca

SUBSTITUTES TO TRY Homemade Barbecue Sauce (page 123), homemade tapenade, homemade dressings, balsamic vinegar, and capers

 # WHEAT

FOODS TO AVOID All whole wheat grains (including spelt, farro, wheat berries, bulgur, einkorn, kamut, and farina), wheat flours (such as semolina and durum), and processed wheat (such as seitan, pasta, couscous, breads, and baked goods)

UNEXPECTED SOURCES dressings, mustards, sauces, oats, burgers and meatballs, soy sauce, matzo meal, cereal, processed meats, modified food starch, malt, and MSG

SUBSTITUTES TO TRY Allergy-free 1-to-1 flour mixes, cornmeal, corn or tapioca starch, certified gluten-free oats and oat flour, rice and corn noodles, salt (in place of MSG), gluten-free bread crumbs, quinoa, and rice

 # SOY

FOODS TO AVOID Edamame (whole soybeans), soy sauce, soy oil, soya, soy lecithin, miso, soy protein, hydrolyzed soy protein, soy flour, soy milk, natto, tempeh, tofu, tamari, and any other product derived from soybeans

UNEXPECTED SOURCES bottled sauces and dressings, packaged foods (both sweet and savory), chips, crackers, shortening, fried foods, frozen foods, plant-based protein powders, plant-based milks, plant-based ice creams, breads, margarine, vegan butters, and vegan cheeses

SUBSTITUTES TO TRY Canola oil, sunflower oil, avocado oil, rice milk, oat milk, lard, hemp protein powder, shredded seaweed, apple cider vinegar, and balsamic vinegar (to replace soy sauce)

 # TREE NUTS

FOODS TO AVOID Brazil nuts, hazelnuts, chestnuts, almonds, pistachios, walnuts, cashews, macadamia nuts, pine nuts, all other tree nuts, coconut, nut flours, nut butters, nut oils, and nut milks

UNEXPECTED SOURCES sauces such as pesto, baked goods and pastries (such as macarons and croissants), marzipan, salads, soups, stews, marinades, dressings, chocolate, plant-based cheeses, granola bars, trail mix, and mortadella

SUBSTITUTES TO TRY Seeds, seed butters, seed oils (such as flax), plant-based milks (such as oat and hemp), and legumes

 # PEANUTS

FOODS TO AVOID Whole and chopped peanuts, peanut butter, peanut oil, peanut flour, and peanut milk

UNEXPECTED SOURCES pastries and baked goods, candies, chocolate, taffy, ice cream and other frozen treats, bottled sauces and dressings, granola and cereals, trail mix, protein powder, and protein bars

SUBSTITUTES TO TRY Shelled sunflower seeds, sunflower seed butter, pumpkin seeds, pumpkin seed butter, granola butter, tahini, avocado oil, and canola oil

A great substitute for peanut products is shelled sunflower seeds and sunflower seed butter, which has a slightly nutty taste and a very similar texture to peanut butter. Pumpkin seeds, pumpkin seed butter, granola butter, and tahini are also effective alternatives. Instead of peanut oil, try avocado oil, which has a high smoke point, or canola oil, which has a neutral flavor.

The Allergy-Free Pantry

Having commonly used allergy-free staples on hand will make cooking and baking so much simpler and faster. Here are nine items that I keep stocked in my pantry and that are used in many recipes in this book.

Allergy-free chocolate: This chocolate is fun to add to granola, muffins, pancakes, and banana bread, or just to eat as a snack. Stock regular, semisweet, and dark chocolate.

Apple cider vinegar: This versatile ingredient can be used in sweet and savory recipes. It adds rise to baked goods and has a rich and distinctive flavor that adds umami to savory dishes.

Chia seeds: Chia seeds are an excellent egg substitute when mixed with water and a great addition to breakfast foods, such as granola and cereal, and salads for protein.

Chicken or vegetable stock or broth: If there's a commercially available brand that is allergy safe for you, it pays to have stock or broth on hand for many of the recipes in this book. It adds instant flavor. If making homemade stock or broth, store it in your refrigerator or freezer rather than your pantry.

Cocoa powder: An allergy-free pure cocoa powder can be your best friend for dessert, breakfast, and homemade staples, such as chocolate syrup. Be sure to get one that is dairy-free, as not all of them are.

Dried herbs and spices: Dried oregano, ground cinnamon, and ground paprika are used in nearly any marinade, dressing, or sweet recipe.

Gluten-free 1-to-1 flour mix: Mixing flours is the only way to get a truly amazing texture in your gluten-free baked goods. Not all flour mixes are created equal, so when you find one you love, stock up.

Noodles/pasta: Gluten-free noodles made from rice, corn, quinoa, or other allergy-free ingredients are very handy to have in your pantry. Keep a variety of long noodles and short-cut pastas.

Olive oil: Nearly every savory dish in this book calls for extra-virgin olive oil because it is a fabulous substitute for butter. You do not have to buy the most expensive one, just one that is pure.

About the Recipes

Here are some recipe tips you will find throughout the book that help keep your allergy-free cooking easy, fun, and delicious.

- **ALLERGY VARIATION TIP:** Includes optional ingredient variations to make recipes more flexible, such as a variation that uses soy sauce for those who can eat soy

- **FLAVOR BOOST:** Suggests additional ingredients that add more flavor and pizzazz to a recipe

- **INGREDIENT TIP:** Explains how to choose the right ingredients and how to work with them in a particular recipe

- **SUBSTITUTION TIP:** Suggests what to swap out of a recipe to make it vegetarian or sugar-free

You'll also find the following convenience labels to help you choose which recipes to make.

- **5 OR FEWER INGREDIENTS:** The recipe uses 5 ingredients, excluding salt, pepper, and nonstick cooking spray or oil.

- **30 MINUTES OR LESS:** The recipe takes 30 minutes or less from start to finish.

- **ONE-POT:** The recipe makes a complete entrée in which all the main ingredients of the dish are cooked in one pot or pan.

- **VEGAN/VEGETARIAN:** The recipe is either completely free of animal products or meat products.

- **WORTH THE WAIT:** The recipe takes longer than 45 minutes from start to finish.

Let's get started!

Cornmeal Muffins,
page 18

Breakfast

Cornmeal Muffins

Makes 12 medium muffins or 9 large muffins

Prep time: 10 minutes
Cook time: 20 minutes

- 30 Minutes or Less
- Vegan

1 cup water
⅓ cup unsweetened applesauce
1 tablespoon freshly squeezed lemon juice
⅓ cup maple syrup
¼ cup extra-virgin olive, canola, or avocado oil
1 tablespoon chia seeds
1 cup cornmeal
½ cup gluten-free oat flour, plus 1 tablespoon
½ cup gluten-free 1-to-1 flour mix with tapioca starch or xanthan gum
2½ teaspoons baking powder
⅛ teaspoon salt
1 cup fresh mixed berries, patted dry
½ cup allergy-free chocolate chips

Can't pick up a quick muffin at your local coffee shop because of allergens? Freeze these flavorful muffins flat in a freezer-strength bag and defrost as needed.

1. Preheat the oven to 375°F and line a muffin tin with paper liners.

2. In a large bowl, whisk together the water, apple-sauce, lemon juice, maple syrup, and olive oil. Whisk in the chia seeds, then let the mixture sit for 5 minutes, until the seeds are sticky and slimy.

3. Add the cornmeal, ½ cup of oat flour, the flour mix, the baking powder, and the salt, mixing well.

4. Sprinkle the remaining 1 tablespoon of oat flour on top of the batter, then pour the berries and chocolate chips on top, folding them in. This will prevent the berries from sinking to the bottom of the muffins.

5. Spoon the batter equally into the prepared muffin cups. Bake for 16 to 18 minutes, or until a toothpick inserted in the center comes out clean.

Ingredient Tip: When working with gluten-free flours, mixing is important. You need a gluten-free flour mix that contains a combination of grains and starches to create a light, fluffy texture. Xanthan gum and tapioca starch are excellent binding and textural agents. Single-ingredient gluten-free flours result in dense baked goods. Avoid mixes that contain almond meal, soy flour, or other top allergens.

Per Serving: (1 medium muffin): Calories: 192; Total fat: 8g; Sodium: 232mg; Carbohydrates: 27g; Fiber: 3g; Protein: 3g

"Nutty" Oat Bars

Makes 12 bars
Prep time: 10 minutes
Cook time: 15 minutes

- 30 Minutes or Less
- Vegan

2 bananas
⅓ cup sunflower seed
   butter
1½ cups gluten-free
   oats
½ teaspoon ground
   cinnamon
½ cup puffed rice
   cereal
⅛ teaspoon salt
⅓ cup allergy-free
   chocolate chunks

Take your morning oatmeal and banana on the go with these flavorful bars. Wrap servings individually and store in the refrigerator to keep them firm and fresh for up to three days. With good-for-you ingredients and no added sugar, these bars will become a breakfast staple in no time.

1. Preheat the oven to 375°F and line an 8-inch square cake pan or baking dish with parchment paper.

2. In a medium bowl, mash the bananas until mostly smooth (a few little chunks are fine).

3. Add the sunflower seed butter and mix well.

4. Add the oats, cinnamon, rice cereal, salt, and chocolate chunks, mixing until well combined.

5. Press the mixture into the prepared pan and spread it out evenly. It should not be loosely sitting in the pan; press it in using your fingers or a fork.

6. Bake for 10 to 12 minutes, or until the mixture is golden brown on top and set.

7. Let the bars cool completely, then use a sharp knife to slice into 12 bars.

Flavor Boost: Add 1 tablespoon of allergy-free pure cocoa powder to the bowl before mixing all of the ingredients together for an extra-chocolaty oat bar.

Per Serving: (1 bar): Calories: 141; Total fat: 7g; Sodium: 28mg; Carbohydrates: 17g; Fiber: 3g; Protein: 4g

Chocolate Chip Banana Bread

Makes 1 loaf
Prep time: 10 minutes
Cook time: 40 minutes

- Vegan
- Worth the Wait

1½ cups mashed banana

¼ cup extra-virgin olive, canola, or avocado oil

¼ cup maple syrup

¼ cup brown sugar

2 tablespoons apple cider vinegar or white vinegar

1½ tablespoons chia seeds

½ teaspoon pure vanilla extract

1¾ cups gluten-free oat flour

1¼ cups gluten-free 1-to-1 flour mix

2 teaspoons baking powder

1 teaspoon baking soda

⅛ teaspoon salt

½ cup allergy-free chocolate chips

Your afternoon tea is about to get the perfect complement with this tender, fluffy chocolate chip banana bread. Compared to commercial baked goods, this banana bread is lower in sugar and made with simple whole food ingredients.

1. Preheat the oven to 375°F and line a loaf pan with parchment paper.

2. In a large bowl, mix together the banana, oil, maple syrup, brown sugar, vinegar, chia seeds, and vanilla.

3. Add the oat flour, flour mix, baking powder, baking soda, and salt, mixing until just combined. Fold in the chocolate chips.

4. Transfer the batter to the prepared pan and gently even out the top with a spatula or spoon.

5. Bake for 35 to 40 minutes, or until a toothpick inserted in the center comes out clean.

Ingredient Tip: When selecting chocolate, go for one with a clear allergy-free claim on the package. That is the best way to ensure that the company takes measures to avoid cross contamination during processing.

Per Serving: (¹⁄₁₂ loaf): Calories: 305; Total fat: 11g; Sodium: 223mg; Carbohydrates: 48g; Fiber: 4g; Protein: 5g

Bacon and Potato Hash

Serves 4
Prep time: 5 minutes
Cook time: 20 minutes

- ■ **5 or Fewer Ingredients**
- ■ **30 Minutes or Less**
- ■ **One-Pot**

5 bacon slices, cut into ½-inch chunks
5 cups finely chopped yellow potatoes (skins on)
½ cup finely chopped or shredded onion
½ teaspoon paprika
¼ teaspoon freshly ground black pepper
Salt

A one-pan breakfast made for lazy weekend mornings. If you're looking for an indulgent egg-free dish with traditional breakfast food components, this is the answer. Tender, golden, and crispy hash browns are combined with golden-brown bacon for a recipe reminiscent of a diner meal.

1. In a large nonstick skillet with a lid over medium-low heat, cook the bacon until translucent, for 3 to 5 minutes.

2. Add the potatoes and onion on top, cover, and increase the heat to medium. Cook for 10 minutes, then uncover and stir in the paprika, pepper, and salt. Cover and cook for another 5 minutes, until the potatoes are tender and the bacon is cooked through.

3. Uncover, increase the heat to medium-high, and cook, stirring often with a spatula, for 2 to 3 minutes, or until the hash is browned to your liking.

4. Taste and add salt as needed, then serve.

Flavor Boost: Before serving, garnish the top of the skillet with chopped scallions or chives, a splash of apple cider vinegar, and your favorite allergy-free ketchup or hot sauce.

Substitution Tip: To make this dish vegetarian, replace the bacon with half a can of drained and rinsed red kidney beans and 3 tablespoons of extra-virgin olive oil.

Per Serving: Calories: 220; Total fat: 5g; Sodium: 293mg; Carbohydrates: 35g; Fiber: 5g; Protein: 9g

Banana Waffles with Fresh Fruit

**Makes 6
(5-inch) waffles
Prep time:** 10 minutes
Cook time: 10 minutes

- 30 Minutes or Less
- Vegan

⅓ cup mashed banana

⅓ cup rice milk or
   gluten-free oat milk

2 teaspoons canola
   or avocado oil, plus
   more for greasing

½ teaspoon apple
   cider vinegar or
   white vinegar

1 tablespoon brown
   sugar

⅛ teaspoon salt

¾ cup gluten-free
   1-to-1 flour mix with
   tapioca starch or
   xanthan gum

½ teaspoon baking
   powder

¼ teaspoon baking
   soda

Allergy-free buttery
   spread

Maple syrup

Seasonal fruit

Make a big batch of these golden, fluffy waffles and freeze them flat for quick breakfasts that your future self will thank you for. Defrost them in the oven for a crunchy exterior.

1. In a medium bowl, whisk together the banana, rice milk, canola oil, vinegar, brown sugar, and salt until smooth. Mix in the flour mix, baking powder, and baking soda. Let the batter stand for 3 to 5 minutes so bubbles can form.

2. Grease a mini waffle maker with some oil. (You will likely need to regrease between waffles.) Spoon in about ¼ cup of batter (for a standard mini waffle maker), then cook according to your machine's directions. If you prefer your waffle extra crispy, flip the waffle over and cook again on the other side.

3. Serve the waffles with buttery spread, maple syrup, and seasonal fruit.

Allergy Variation Tip: Is banana a no-go in your home? Simply replace the mashed banana with the same amount of unsweetened applesauce.

Per Serving: (1 waffle): Calories: 106; Total fat: 2g; Sodium: 137mg; Carbohydrates: 21g; Fiber: 1g; Protein: 1g

Pancakes with Caramelized Apples

Makes 6 (5-inch) pancakes
Prep time: 10 minutes
Cook time: 20 minutes

- 30 Minutes or Less
- Vegan

⅓ cup gluten-free oat milk, rice milk, or water

⅓ cup unsweetened applesauce

2 tablespoons brown sugar

1 teaspoon apple cider or white vinegar

⅛ teaspoon salt

½ cup gluten-free 1-to-1 flour mix with tapioca starch or xanthan gum

1 teaspoon baking powder

½ teaspoon baking soda

2 teaspoons avocado or canola oil

1 apple, cored and chopped or sliced

1 tablespoon allergy-free buttery spread (optional)

2 tablespoons maple syrup

Instead of garnishing pancakes with cake-like toppings, these flavorful apples are a whole food topping that contributes fiber (just don't peel the skin). They only take a couple of minutes to cook.

1. In a medium bowl, whisk together the oat milk, applesauce, brown sugar, vinegar, and salt. Whisk in the flour mix, baking powder, and baking soda until just combined. Let the batter stand for 3 to 5 minutes so bubbles can form.

2. In a large nonstick skillet over medium heat, warm the avocado oil. Work in two batches, using a ¼-cup measure to add the batter. Cook for 2 to 3 minutes, until bubbles form and pop, then flip. Cook for 2 to 3 minutes more on the other side, then transfer to a plate.

3. In the same skillet over medium heat, cook the apples and buttery spread (if using), stirring often, for 5 to 7 minutes, or until browned. Add the maple syrup at the very end just to warm it. Pour the syrupy apples over the pancakes and serve.

Allergy Variation Tip: If you are not allergic to dairy, add butter to the hot pancakes before serving.

Flavor Boost: Hit the pancakes and apples with cinnamon before serving.

Per Serving: (1 pancake): Calories: 118; Total fat: 2g; Sodium: 220mg; Carbohydrates: 25g; Fiber: 1g; Protein: 1g

Carrot and Spice Dollar Pancakes

Makes
20 to 24 dollar-size pancakes
Prep time: 10 minutes
Cook time: 30 minutes

■ Vegan

½ cup grated carrot
⅓ cup unsweetened
  applesauce
¼ cup water
2 tablespoons brown
  sugar
1 tablespoon freshly
  squeezed lemon juice
⅛ teaspoon salt
¾ cup gluten-free
  1-to-1 flour mix with
  tapioca starch or
  xanthan gum
1 teaspoon baking
  powder
½ teaspoon baking
  soda
½ teaspoon pumpkin
  spice mix
2 teaspoons avocado
  or canola oil
Allergy-free buttery
  spread
Maple syrup

When you want carrot cake (and you want it now), make these pancakes. If you have kids who are picky eaters, this recipe is a gentle way to introduce veggies without them being the star of the show.

1. In a large bowl, whisk together the carrot, applesauce, water, brown sugar, lemon juice, and salt. Add the flour mix, baking powder, baking soda, and spice mix, whisking until just combined.

2. In a large nonstick skillet over medium heat, warm the avocado oil. Working in 4 to 5 batches, add dollar-size dollops of batter and cook for 2 to 3 minutes, until bubbles form and leave dimples. Flip and cook for another 2 to 3 minutes.

3. Serve with buttery spread and maple syrup.

Ingredient Tip: If you don't have pumpkin spice mix, combine ¼ teaspoon of cinnamon, ⅛ teaspoon of ground cloves, and ⅛ teaspoon of ground ginger.

Substitution Tip: To make the recipe sugar-free, omit the brown sugar. The pancakes will be slightly less golden brown in color.

Per Serving: (5 pancakes): Calories: 171; Total fat: 3g; Sodium: 338mg; Carbohydrates: 35g; Fiber: 1g; Protein: 2g

Chocolate Fudge Chia Pudding

Serves 4
Prep time: 30 minutes

- 30 Minutes or Less
- One-Pot
- Vegan

¼ cup chia seeds
¼ cup maple syrup
2 tablespoons cocoa powder
1 tablespoon sunflower seed butter
½ teaspoon vanilla
Pinch salt
1¼ cups rice milk or gluten-free oat milk (preferably a barista style)

This healthy, protein-rich pudding feels more like a dessert than a breakfast with the combination of seeds, vanilla, and chocolate. It is sweetened naturally with maple syrup. Serve it on its own or with your favorite fresh or frozen berries.

1. In a reusable lidded jar, whisk together the chia seeds, maple syrup, cocoa powder, sunflower seed butter, vanilla, and salt until the mixture is smooth with no lumps.

2. Slowly add the rice milk, whisking until smooth after each addition.

3. Let the mixture stand for 25 minutes, stirring every few minutes. The chia seeds will puff up as they absorb the liquid, making the pudding creamy and thick.

4. Spoon into cups to serve or cover and store in the refrigerator overnight for a quick breakfast tomorrow. If the pudding tightens up too much in the refrigerator, loosen it with another tablespoon or two of rice milk.

Allergy Variation Tip: If you are not allergic to coconut, swap out the rice or oat milk for 1 cup of low-fat coconut milk or coconut drink.

Per Serving: Calories: 174; Total fat: 7g; Sodium: 76mg; Carbohydrates: 25g; Fiber: 6g; Protein: 6g

Red Berry Oatmeal

Serves 2
Prep time: 2 minutes
Cook time: 10 minutes

- 5 or Fewer Ingredients
- 30 Minutes or Less
- Vegan

2 cups water
1 cup gluten-free oats
1 cup sliced
  fresh stemmed
  strawberries
½ cup fresh
  raspberries
2 tablespoons maple
  syrup, plus more for
  drizzling
⅛ teaspoon salt
Allergy-free buttery
  spread or coconut oil,
  for serving (optional)

This beautiful oatmeal is bursting with flavor and has a gorgeous creamy texture. The berries give it a nice pale pink color and also contribute nutritional benefits, like fiber and vitamins.

1. In a medium pot over medium heat, combine the water, oats, strawberries, raspberries, maple syrup, and salt. Cook, stirring often, for 5 to 7 minutes until thickened. Cook for 2 to 3 minutes more, stirring constantly.

2. Serve drizzled with maple syrup and add buttery spread (if using).

Ingredient Tip: When selecting oats, always look for the Purity Protocol gluten-free label. While oats are not innately glutinous, they are cross-contaminated with wheat during processing. If the label does not ensure they are tested and gluten-free, then they are not gluten-free. This applies to any oat product, including oat milk and oat flour.

Per Serving: Calories: 277; Total fat: 4g; Sodium: 160mg; Carbohydrates: 54g; Fiber: 9g; Protein: 9g

Maple-Cinnamon Granola

Serves 4
Prep time: 10 minutes
Cook time: 10 minutes

- 30 Minutes or Less
- Vegan

1¼ cups gluten-free
  oats
¾ cup puffed rice
  cereal
¼ cup shelled pumpkin
  seeds
1 tablespoon flaxseed
1 teaspoon ground
  cinnamon
⅛ teaspoon salt
¼ cup maple syrup
½ teaspoon pure
  vanilla extract

It can be difficult and expensive to find an allergy-free brand of granola. Fortunately, it is super easy to make your own at home. Eat it as a snack or add it to smoothie bowls or cultured yogurt. The pumpkin seeds (whether salted or unsalted, raw or roasted) offer zinc as well as lean protein.

1. Preheat the oven to 375°F and line a baking sheet with parchment paper.

2. In a medium bowl, combine the oats, rice cereal, pumpkin seeds, flaxseed, cinnamon, and salt and mix well. Add the maple syrup and vanilla, mixing until evenly coated.

3. Transfer the mixture to the prepared baking sheet, spreading evenly and allowing some clumps to form without it being piled into a mound. Bake for 8 to 10 minutes, until golden brown. Keep a close watch during the last 2 minutes, as granola can burn quickly.

4. Allow the granola to cool, then transfer it to an airtight container.

Ingredient Tip: When selecting a puffed rice cereal, ensure it is both allergy-free and gluten-free. Although rice does not contain wheat gluten, cereals can be cross-contaminated with gluten or other allergens during processing.

Per Serving: Calories: 227; Total fat: 6g; Sodium: 100mg; Carbohydrates: 36g; Fiber: 5g; Protein: 7g

Panfried Potatoes,
page 36

Snacks and Sides

Crunchy Seed Crackers

Serves 6
Prep time: 15 minutes
Cook time: 20 minutes

- 5 or Fewer Ingredients
- Vegetarian

1¾ cups gluten-free
  1-to-1 flour mix, plus
  more for dusting
3 tablespoons flaxseed
1 teaspoon salt, plus
  more as needed
1 teaspoon freshly
  ground black pepper
½ cup water
¼ cup extra-virgin
  olive oil or flaxseed
  oil, divided
2 tablespoons honey
  or maple syrup

Making crackers at home is surprisingly easy. These crackers include flaxseed, which is rich in omega-3s and adds a pleasant crunch and "nutty" taste to the dough.

1. Preheat the oven to 450°F and line a baking sheet with parchment paper.

2. In a large bowl, whisk together the flour mix, flaxseed, salt, and pepper.

3. Make a well in the center and add the water, 3 tablespoons of olive oil, and the honey. Whisk the wet ingredients together in the center of the well, then slowly bring in the dry ingredients until it forms a ball of dough. Knead the dough by folding it over on itself, then pressing down, for 10 folds. This creates layers in the dough.

4. On the prepared baking sheet, roll the dough into a 10-by-14-inch rectangle, making sure the thickness is even. Brush the remaining 1 tablespoon of olive oil on top, then sprinkle on some salt. Prick the dough all over with a fork. With a smooth knife, cut the dough into 4 rows of 6 crackers. Do not separate the individual crackers.

5. Bake for 15 minutes, then remove the sheet and separate the crackers using a spatula. Bake for another 2 to 4 minutes, until the edges brown.

6. Let cool completely before handling, then serve.

Flavor Boost: Add chopped fresh rosemary and garlic to the cracker dough before kneading.

Per Serving: (4 crackers): Calories: 284; Total fat: 11g; Sodium: 390mg; Carbohydrates: 42g; Fiber: 2g; Protein: 3g

Strawberry-Basil Salsa

Serves 4
Prep time: 10 minutes

- 5 or Fewer Ingredients
- 30 Minutes or Less
- Vegan

1½ cups fresh chopped, stemmed strawberries
¼ cup extra-virgin olive oil
2 tablespoons freshly squeezed lemon or lime juice
10 large basil leaves, chopped
1 shallot, finely chopped (about 2 tablespoons)
1 garlic clove, chopped (about 1 teaspoon)
Salt
Freshly ground black pepper

This simple salsa tastes more colorful with every bite. Dunk Crunchy Seed Crackers (page 32), tortilla chips, or sliced cucumber into it, or spoon it onto grilled chicken for a savory light lunch.

1. In a large bowl, combine the strawberries, olive oil, lemon juice, basil, shallot, and garlic. Taste and add salt and pepper as needed.

2. Transfer to a serving bowl and enjoy.

Ingredient Tip: This recipe is even more flavorful when strawberries are in season.

Per Serving: Calories: 144; Total fat: 14g; Sodium: 2mg; Carbohydrates: 6g; Fiber: 1g; Protein: 1g

Peppery Kale Chips

Serves 4
Prep time: 5 minutes
Cook time: 10 minutes

- 5 or Fewer Ingredients
- 30 Minutes or Less
- Vegan

---

1 head kale, stemmed (about 5 cups)
3 tablespoons extra-virgin olive oil
1 teaspoon paprika
½ teaspoon salt
½ teaspoon freshly ground black pepper

Kale chips are crunchy, satisfying, and a nutritious alternative to potato chips. Plus, they can be made at home with little to no mess or time commitment. Kale is full of fiber, antioxidants, and vitamins, and its rough texture holds up well to roasting at high temperatures, making perfectly crisp chips.

1. Preheat the oven to 400°F and line a baking sheet with parchment paper.

2. Wash the kale leaves and spin to dry. Dry leaves result in crispier chips.

3. Transfer the kale leaves to the prepared baking sheet, then drizzle on the olive oil, tossing to coat with your hands. Evenly spread the leaves out on the sheet.

4. Evenly sprinkle the paprika, salt, and pepper on top.

5. Bake for 8 to 10 minutes, or until the kale leaves are crispy and browned. Let cool before serving.

Flavor Boost: Season the kale with 2 teaspoons of nutritional yeast for a dairy-free, cheese-like umami flavor.

Per Serving: Calories: 101; Total fat: 10g; Sodium: 299mg; Carbohydrates: 2g; Fiber: 1g; Protein: 1g

Panfried Potatoes

Serves 4
Prep time: 10 minutes
Cook time: 25 minutes

- **5 or Fewer Ingredients**
- **One-Pot**
- **Vegan**

3 tablespoons extra-virgin olive oil
1½ pounds mini potatoes, halved
Salt
Freshly ground black pepper
2 cups lightly packed chopped kale
2 cups shredded red cabbage
½ cup sliced onion
2 tablespoons apple cider vinegar

Crispy potatoes are delicious, but crispy potatoes with earthy greens and colorful cabbage are even better. The apple cider vinegar adds a subtle umami flavor to balance out the dish, as well as beneficial probiotic cultures, so long as you use a brand that contains the mother culture in the bottle.

1. In a large nonstick skillet with a lid over high heat, warm the olive oil.

2. Add the potatoes, season with salt and pepper, and fry for 2 minutes. Reduce the heat to medium, cover, and cook for 15 minutes, until fork-tender and lightly golden brown.

3. Uncover and add the kale, cabbage, and onion, mixing well. Fry for another 5 minutes, until the vegetables are wilted and soft.

4. Drizzle the vinegar on top, season well with salt and pepper, and serve.

Flavor Boost: Serve with your favorite allergy-free ketchup or hot sauce.

Per Serving: Calories: 246; Total fat: 10g; Sodium: 65mg; Carbohydrates: 35g; Fiber: 5g; Protein: 5g

Garlicky White Bean Dip

Serves 6
Prep time: 5 minutes
Cook time: 20 minutes

- 5 or Fewer Ingredients
- 30 Minutes or Less
- Vegan

1 (15.5-ounce) can of white kidney beans, drained and well rinsed
5 garlic cloves, peeled and left whole
½ cup extra-virgin olive oil, divided
Salt
Freshly ground black pepper
Leaves of 1 rosemary sprig
2 tablespoons freshly squeezed lemon juice

This luxurious bean dip is shockingly easy to make. Roasting the ingredients first enhances all of their natural flavors and adds complexity to the dish. Serve with Crunchy Seed Crackers (page 32), or serve as a protein with vegetarian dishes. While the dip is still warm, toss with hot allergy-free pasta for a deliciously creamy sauce.

1. Preheat the oven to 375°F and line a baking sheet with parchment paper.

2. Place the beans and garlic on the prepared baking sheet. Drizzle 1 tablespoon of olive oil onto the beans and garlic, and season with salt and pepper. Bake for 15 to 18 minutes, or until the beans are golden brown.

3. When cool enough to handle, transfer the beans and garlic to a food processor. Add the remaining olive oil, the rosemary, and the lemon juice. Taste and add salt and pepper as needed. Blend until smooth, then transfer to a serving bowl and enjoy.

Ingredient Tip: Use purple garlic as opposed to white garlic whenever possible. Purple garlic has a superior flavor and texture. Always avoid pre-peeled or pre-chopped garlic.

Per Serving: Calories: 220; Total fat: 18g; Sodium: 27mg; Carbohydrates: 11g; Fiber: 3g; Protein: 4g

Crispy Shaved Brussels Sprouts

Serves 4
Prep time: 10 minutes
Cook time: 10 minutes

- 5 or Fewer Ingredients
- 30 Minutes or Less
- One-Pot
- Vegan

3 tablespoons extra-virgin olive oil
3 cups shaved or thinly sliced Brussels sprouts
Salt
Freshly ground black pepper
2 tablespoons apple cider vinegar

A few ingredients with so much zest. This recipe comes together quickly (even more so if you shave the sprouts in a food processor) and complements nearly any dish. Brussels sprouts are not just for the holidays; enjoy them year-round with this simple side dish.

1. In a large nonstick skillet over high heat, warm the olive oil.

2. Add the Brussels sprouts to the skillet and season with salt and pepper. Sauté, tossing the sprouts every minute or so to prevent burning, for 5 to 7 minutes, or until they are wilted with lots of crispy bits.

3. Remove the skillet from the heat and pour in the vinegar, mixing well. Taste and add salt and pepper as needed, then serve.

Allergen Variation: If you are not allergic to dairy, exclude the vinegar and add grated Parmesan cheese before serving.

Per Serving: Calories: 119; Total fat: 10g; Sodium: 56mg; Carbohydrates: 6g; Fiber: 3g; Protein: 2g

Warm Olives

Serves 4
Prep time: 5 minutes
Cook time: 15 minutes

- 5 or Fewer Ingredients
- 30 Minutes or Less
- Vegan

1 (6-ounce) can pitted black or green olives
¼ cup extra-virgin olive oil
2 tablespoons freshly squeezed lemon juice
1 teaspoon red pepper flakes or chopped hot chile
1 celery stalk, thinly sliced

Olives not only have a satisfying savory flavor but also contain good fats that are beneficial for your body, as well as antioxidants. The fresh and bitter flavors of celery and lemon juice perfectly complement the flavor of the olives.

1. Preheat the oven to 375°F.

2. In a small oven-safe metal skillet or baking dish, combine the olives, olive oil, lemon juice, red pepper flakes, and celery, mixing well.

3. Bake for 15 minutes, or until everything is soft and tender.

4. Serve as an appetizer or as an accompaniment to your favorite savory dish.

Flavor Boost: Add the leaves from 1 sprig of fresh oregano, or 2 teaspoons of dried oregano, before baking.

Per Serving: Calories: 173; Total fat: 19g; Sodium: 555mg; Carbohydrates: 2g; Fiber: 1g; Protein: 0g

Mashed Potatoes

Serves 4
Prep time: 5 minutes
Cook time: 25 Minutes

- ■ **5 or Fewer Ingredients**
- ■ **30 Minutes or Less**
- ■ **Vegan**

6 yellow potatoes, skins on, halved

5 garlic cloves, peeled and left whole

¼ cup extra-virgin olive oil

2 tablespoons Dijon mustard

¼ cup chopped fresh chives

Salt

It's commonly thought that a good mashed potato recipe requires a lot of butter and milk. But that is false. You can make incredible mashed potatoes without any dairy at all and flavor them with other herbs and spices.

1. In a medium pot, cover the potatoes with water by about an inch. Bring to a boil over high heat, then boil for 15 to 18 minutes, or until the potatoes are fork-tender. Add the garlic during the last 8 to 10 minutes.

2. Reserve ¼ cup of the boiling liquid. Drain the potatoes, then use a fork to carefully remove the skins, which should have loosened and begun to fall off while boiling.

3. With a dinner fork or a potato masher, mash the potatoes. Add 2 tablespoons of the reserved liquid, the olive oil, the mustard, and the chives, mixing well. Add more of the reserved liquid a bit at a time, as needed. Taste and add salt as needed, then serve.

Ingredient Tip: Some brands of Dijon mustard contain wheat gluten. If this is one of your allergens or intolerances, be sure to look for a wheat- and gluten-free mustard.

Per Serving: Calories: 376; Total fat: 14g; Sodium: 145mg; Carbohydrates: 58g; Fiber: 8g; Protein: 7g

Dill and Cucumber Salad

Serves 4
Prep time: 10 minutes

- ■ **5 or Fewer Ingredients**
- ■ **30 Minutes or Less**
- ■ **One-Pot**
- ■ **Vegan**

2 shallots, thinly sliced, or ¼ cup thinly sliced red onion

1 English cucumber, thinly sliced (about 4 cups)

1 bunch fresh dill, finely chopped (about ½ cup)

⅓ cup extra-virgin olive oil

¼ cup freshly squeezed lemon juice

1 tablespoon finely chopped garlic

1 teaspoon freshly ground black pepper

Salt

If you love herby, garlicky salads, this one's for you. Refreshing cucumber and lemon juice are grounded by deep green dill, a thin-leafed herb that is said to have many health benefits in addition to a nice fragrance.

In a large bowl, combine the shallots, cucumber, dill, olive oil, lemon juice, garlic, and pepper, mixing well. Taste and add salt as needed, then serve.

Ingredient Tip: English cucumbers work best for this recipe because of their mild flavor, even texture, and thin skin. If using another variety of cucumber, you may need to peel the skin and remove the seeds; for pickling cucumbers, you will have to cut off the bitter ends as they spoil the flavor of the salad.

Per Serving: Calories: 178; Total fat: 18g; Sodium: 119mg; Carbohydrates: 5g; Fiber: 1g; Protein: 1g

Balsamic-Roasted Carrots

Serves 4
Prep time: 5 minutes
Cook time: 25 minutes

- 5 or Fewer Ingredients
- 30 Minutes or Less
- Vegetarian

5 or 6 carrots,
  diagonally sliced
  ½ inch thick (about
  3 cups)
1 tablespoon
  extra-virgin olive oil
1 tablespoon balsamic
  vinegar
1 tablespoon honey
Salt
Freshly ground black
  pepper

With fiber, beta-carotene, and that perfect meaty crunch, carrots get an upgrade with sweet and savory balsamic vinegar and honey.

1. Preheat the oven to 375°F and line a baking sheet with parchment paper.

2. Place the carrots onto the prepared baking sheet. Combine the olive oil, vinegar, and honey in a small bowl or measuring cup. Drizzle the mixture over the carrots, tossing to coat evenly. Taste and add salt and pepper as needed.

3. Roast for 15 minutes, then remove the baking sheet from the oven. Flip the carrots and turn the oven up to 400°F. Roast for 10 minutes more, until the edges of the carrots are golden brown.

Substitution Tip: Swap the honey for an equal amount of maple syrup to make the recipe vegan.

Per Serving: Calories: 89; Total fat: 4g; Sodium: 106mg; Carbohydrates: 14g; Fiber: 3g; Protein: 1g

Mixed Greens with Apple and Endive

Serves 4
Prep time: 10 minutes

- 30 Minutes or Less
- Vegan

½ head lettuce of
choice
½ head lettuce of
choice
1 head endive, cut into
1-inch-wide slices
1 apple, cored and
thinly sliced
½ cup extra-virgin
olive oil
¼ cup apple cider
vinegar
1 garlic clove, minced
½ teaspoon freshly
ground black pepper
Salt

Sweet, fibrous apples, bitter endive, and nutritious lettuces are perfectly balanced in this salad, a great accompaniment to nearly any main dish. Choose two different kinds of lettuce, such as Boston and red leaf lettuce.

1. In a large salad bowl, combine the two types of lettuce, endive, and apple. Set aside.

2. In a small bowl, whisk together the olive oil, vinegar, garlic, and pepper. Season with salt.

3. Drizzle the dressing over the salad and toss well, then serve.

Ingredient Tip: Boston lettuce and red leaf lettuce work best in this recipe because of their fluffy texture and mild flavor.

Per Serving: Calories: 307; Total fat: 27g; Sodium: 82mg; Carbohydrates: 15g; Fiber: 7g; Protein: 3g

Pepper and Onion Stir-Fry

Serves 4
Prep time: 5 minutes
Cook time: 15 minutes

- 5 or Fewer Ingredients
- 30 Minutes or Less
- Vegan

2 tablespoons extra-virgin olive oil
2 garlic cloves, finely chopped (about 1 tablespoon)
½ onion, thinly sliced (about 1 cup)
Salt
Freshly ground black pepper
2 bell peppers, cut into strips
1 teaspoon paprika
Juice of 1 lime

Get your vitamin C with a healthy dose of caramelized onions, sour lime juice, and toasty paprika. This foolproof stir-fry is saucy and bright.

1. In a large nonstick skillet over medium-low heat, combine the olive oil, garlic, and onion and cook for about 5 minutes, until the onion is soft and translucent. Season with salt and pepper.

2. Add the bell peppers, increase the heat to medium, and cook, stirring often, for 8 to 10 minutes, until lightly browned.

3. Add the paprika and lime juice and toss well. Serve warm.

Flavor Boost: Add a handful of fresh cilantro, coarsely chopped or torn, red pepper flakes, chili powder, or chopped fresh chiles as desired.

Per Serving: Calories: 97; Total fat: 7g; Sodium: 42mg; Carbohydrates: 9g; Fiber: 1g; Protein: 1g

Herbed Quinoa

Serves 4
Prep time: 5 minutes
Cook time: 20 minutes

- ■ 5 or Fewer
  Ingredients
- ■ 30 Minutes or Less
- ■ One-Pot
- ■ Vegan

---

1 cup quinoa
1¼ cups water
¼ cup extra-virgin
  olive oil
1 tablespoon dried
  oregano
1 cup finely chopped
  fresh parsley
1 cup finely chopped
  fresh basil

Use red or white quinoa in this dish (or a bit of both). Quinoa has a reputation for being boring, but it absolutely is not. You just have to know how to dress it up. It is regarded as one of the healthiest foods you can eat, and for good reason. It is rich in amino acids, protein, and many other essential vitamins and minerals.

1. In a medium saucepan over high heat, combine the quinoa and water. Bring to a boil. Cover, reduce the heat to low, and simmer for 15 minutes, until the quinoa is cooked through and the water is absorbed.

2. Fluff with a fork, then add the olive oil, oregano, parsley, and basil. Mix well, then serve.

Flavor Boost: At the end, fold in 2 tablespoons of freshly squeezed lemon juice and/or 2 tablespoons of gluten-free Dijon mustard.

Per Serving: Calories: 285; Total fat: 16g; Sodium: 11mg; Carbohydrates: 29g; Fiber: 4g; Protein: 7g

Tangy Apple and Cabbage Slaw

Serves 4
Prep time: 10 minutes

- ■ 5 or Fewer
  Ingredients
- ■ 30 Minutes or Less
- ■ Vegetarian

3 cups shaved red
  cabbage
2 cups thinly sliced
  apple (preferably a
  crunchy apple such
  as Gala, Granny
  Smith, or Fuji)
1 cup thinly sliced
  celery
⅓ cup extra-virgin
  olive oil
¼ cup apple cider
  vinegar
3 tablespoons honey
  or maple syrup
1 teaspoon salt
½ teaspoon freshly
  ground black pepper

A quick slaw with the right amount of sweetness and tang. Apples and cabbage are two common and inexpensive ingredients with relatively mild flavors. But they can very easily be jazzed up with the right dressing.

1. In a large bowl, combine the cabbage, apple, and celery.

2. In a small bowl or measuring cup, whisk together the olive oil, vinegar, honey, salt, and pepper. Pour the dressing over the slaw mix and toss well.

3. Serve.

Ingredient Tip: Although this is a quick slaw, it is also a great make-ahead recipe, as it fares well in the refrigerator as the flavors marinate together.

Per Serving: Calories: 252; Total fat: 18g; Sodium: 619mg; Carbohydrates: 22g; Fiber: 3g; Protein: 1g

30-Minute
Minestrone, page 54

Vegetarian and Vegan

Creamy Corn Soup

Serves 4
Prep time: 15 minutes
Cook time: 30 minutes

- 5 or Fewer Ingredients
- Vegan
- Worth the Wait

⅓ cup extra-virgin olive oil
4 shallots, sliced
8 ears corn, peeled and kernels sliced off
6 cups vegetable broth
Salt
Freshly ground black pepper

This soup highlights the delicate, sweet flavors of corn. It's particularly delicious when corn is in season, so be sure to take advantage of farm-fresh corn if it is available to you.

1. In a large saucepan over low heat, warm the olive oil. Add the shallots and cook, stirring often, for about 5 minutes, until they are translucent. Add the corn, stir, and cook until the corn turns a darker yellow, about 5 minutes.

2. Add the vegetable broth, increase the heat to high, and bring to a boil. Cook for 20 minutes, or until reduced by about a quarter in volume.

3. Reserve about ⅔ cup of the cooked corn kernels, taking them out of the soup. Using an immersion blender, blend the soup in the saucepan until smooth.

4. Pour the soup into bowls, then swirl in the reserved corn kernels.

5. Season with salt and pepper, then serve.

Allergy Variation Tip: If you are not allergic to coconut, replace 3 cups of vegetable broth with light coconut milk or coconut drink for a richer and thicker soup.

Per Serving: Calories: 410; Total fat: 20g; Sodium: 53mg; Carbohydrates: 60g; Fiber: 7g; Protein: 8g

Spiced Black Beans with Potatoes

Serves 4
Prep time: 10 minutes
Cook time: 25 minutes

- ■ **5 or Fewer Ingredients**
- ■ **Vegan**

3 tablespoons extra-virgin olive oil
4 cups ¼-inch-diced yellow potatoes
1 (15.5-ounce) can black beans, drained and well rinsed
2 teaspoons paprika
1 teaspoon coriander seed
1 teaspoon chili powder
½ teaspoon freshly ground black pepper
Salt

A hit of protein from tender little black beans meets the satisfying crunch of fried potatoes. Both of these key ingredients will help you feel fuller for longer (one of the benefits of starch and fiber), and the spices add a nice kick.

1. In a large nonstick skillet over high heat, warm the olive oil. Add the potatoes and fry for 5 minutes. Reduce the heat to medium-low, cover, and cook for 10 to 12 minutes, or until the potatoes are fork-tender and browned on the bottom.

2. Add the beans, paprika, coriander, chili powder, and pepper. Taste and add salt as needed, mixing well. Increase the heat to medium and cook for another 5 minutes to warm up the beans.

3. Serve.

Flavor Boost: Top the skillet with a dollop of your favorite allergy-free salsa and hot sauce.

Per Serving: Calories: 297; Total fat: 11g; Sodium: 69mg; Carbohydrates: 43g; Fiber: 10g; Protein: 9g

Zoodle Salad

Serves 4
Prep time: 10 minutes

- 5 or Fewer Ingredients
- 30 Minutes or Less
- Vegetarian

½ cup extra-virgin olive oil

¼ cup apple cider vinegar

1 tablespoon grainy mustard

1 tablespoon honey

½ teaspoon salt

½ teaspoon freshly ground black pepper

3 cups spiralized zucchini

3 cups spiralized carrots

Salt

The satisfying twirl of spaghetti, except it's made from raw vegetables. Zoodles are fun to eat, plain and simple. They hold flavor exceptionally well and can be served hot or cold. Get a strong dose of fiber and vitamins from this salad, as well as the pungent fermented goodness of apple cider vinegar and savory grainy mustard.

1. In a large bowl, whisk together the olive oil, vinegar, mustard, honey, salt, and pepper.

2. Add the zucchini and carrots, tossing well.

3. Taste and add salt and pepper as needed, then serve right away.

Ingredient Tip: Spiralized zucchini and carrots that you pick up in the produce section may be convenient, but they cannot match the crunch of freshly spiralized vegetables. Small manual spiralizers can be bought for under $10 and will fit neatly in your utensil drawer. Hand crank or electric spiralizers will create vegetable ribbons at a much faster rate but come with a price tag to match. Once you have spiralized the vegetables, work quickly to assemble the salad, as cut zucchini begins to leak liquid, which will dilute the dressing if it sits for too long.

Per Serving: Calories: 308; Total fat: 28g; Sodium: 399mg; Carbohydrates: 15g; Fiber: 3g; Protein: 2g

30-Minute Minestrone

Serves 4
Prep time: 5 minutes
Cook time: 25 minutes

■ **Vegan**

2 tablespoons
    extra-virgin olive oil
1 large celery stalk,
    sliced (about 1 cup)
1 zucchini, coarsely
    chopped (about
    1 cup)
1 tablespoon tomato
    paste
4 cups vegetable broth
1 cup cherry tomatoes
½ cup shredded
    carrots
1 (15.5-ounce) can
    white kidney beans,
    drained and rinsed
6 ounces allergy-free
    pasta
2½ ounces chard
    leaves or spinach
¼ cup torn fresh
    parsley and basil
Salt
Black pepper

Minestrone is an Italian soup made from veggies, cooking greens, a brothy tomato base, beans, and short noodles. It is incredibly healthy and nutritious and typically enjoyed in the summer, when fresh produce is in season (but, please, enjoy its benefits all year round).

1. In a medium saucepan over medium-high heat, warm the olive oil. Add the celery and zucchini and cook, stirring often, for 5 minutes.

2. Add the tomato paste and mix well. Add the broth, tomatoes, carrots, and beans and bring to a boil. Cook for 20 minutes, adding the pasta toward the end of the cooking process so that it cooks until tender per package instructions. (For example, if the pasta takes 5 minutes to cook, add it after the soup has been boiling for 15 minutes).

3. Stir in the chard, then garnish with the herbs. Taste and add salt and pepper as needed, then serve.

Allergy Variation Tip: If you are not allergic to wheat or do not have celiac disease, use a short-cut traditional wheat pasta or spelt flour pasta.

Per Serving: Calories: 231; Total fat: 8g; Sodium: 140mg; Carbohydrates: 33g; Fiber: 6g; Protein: 9g

Butternut Squash and Flaxseed Soup

Serves 4
Prep time: 10 minutes
Cook time: 25 minutes

- **5 or Fewer Ingredients**
- **One-Pot**
- **Vegan**

¼ cup extra-virgin olive oil
½ cup chopped shallots
Salt
Freshly ground black pepper
¼ cup whole flaxseed
4 cups water
3 cups peeled and cubed butternut squash
1 cup chopped carrots
¼ cup chopped apple

Flaxseed is a great source of omega-3 fatty acids—and is so rarely thought of as a soup ingredient, but the seeds' earthy, slightly nutty profile works well in combination with autumnal butternut squash. Once pureed, the seeds appear as little flecks throughout the soup.

1. In a medium saucepan over medium heat, combine the olive oil and shallot. Cook, stirring often, for 3 to 4 minutes, until fragrant and softened. Season with salt and pepper.

2. Add the flaxseed and mix well. Allow the seeds to toast lightly for 30 seconds, then add the water, squash, carrot, and apple, mixing well. Season with salt and pepper. Increase the heat to high, bring to a boil, then reduce the heat to maintain a simmer for 15 to 20 minutes, until the squash is tender.

3. Puree the soup until smooth using an immersion blender or a heat-safe standing blender. Portion into bowls, then serve.

Flavor Boost: Add a drizzle of flaxseed oil and a sprinkle of flaky sea salt on top of the soup before serving.

Per Serving: Calories: 254; Total fat: 18g; Sodium: 71mg; Carbohydrates: 23g; Fiber: 7g; Protein: 4g

Cauliflower Rice Noodles

Serves 4
Prep time: 10 minutes
Cook time: 20 minutes

- 5 or Fewer Ingredients
- 30 Minutes or Less
- One-Pot
- Vegan

¼ cup extra-virgin olive oil

4 cups small cauliflower florets

1 red or orange bell pepper, cut into ½-inch dice

1 teaspoon ground turmeric

Salt

Freshly ground black pepper

3 cups loosely packed baby spinach

3 cups water

12 ounces rice pasta

Brothy noodles with an abundance of vegetables: the ideal meal for a cozy fall evening. Cauliflower is high in vitamins and aids in healthy digestion. Spinach is rich in iron, an important mineral to keep you energized.

1. In a large nonstick skillet over medium heat, warm the olive oil. Add the cauliflower and bell pepper and cook, stirring often, for 8 to 10 minutes, until the cauliflower has crispy brown bits. Add the turmeric and mix well. Season with salt and pepper.

2. Add the spinach and water. Increase the heat to high, bring to a boil, and add the pasta, mixing well to make sure they are submerged. Cover and cook the pasta until tender according to package instructions. There should be broth remaining in the pan after the pasta is cooked.

3. Taste and add salt and pepper as needed, then serve.

Flavor Boost: Use an equal amount of vegetable broth in place of water for a more complex and indulgent dish.

Per Serving: Calories: 470; Total fat: 16g; Sodium: 93mg; Carbohydrates: 77g; Fiber: 13g; Protein: 10g

One-Pot Pasta with Cherry Tomatoes and Shallots

Serves 4
Prep time: 2 minutes
Cook time: 25 minutes

- 5 or Fewer
  Ingredients
- 30 Minutes or Less
- One-Pot
- Vegan

¼ cup extra-virgin
  olive oil
2 pints cherry or grape
  tomatoes, halved
5 shallots, halved
  lengthwise
2 teaspoons dried
  oregano
Salt
Freshly ground black
  pepper
12 ounces allergy-free
  dried pasta of your
  choosing
2½ cups water

Soft and creamy shallots that melt into the pasta as you scoop it out of the pan—yes please. These small, purplish onions with a slightly garlicky flavor are much softer and less sharp than a typical red onion.

1. In a medium pan over medium-high heat, warm the olive oil.

2. Add the tomatoes and shallot and cook, shaking the pan every few minutes to avoid sticking, for 15 minutes, or until the tomatoes blister and pop and the shallots are golden brown on one side. Try to keep the shallots facedown in the pan and avoid stirring. Add the oregano, then taste and add salt and black pepper as needed.

3. Add the pasta and mix well. Add the water, making sure the pasta is just submerged. Reduce the heat to medium-low, cover, and cook the pasta until tender according to package instructions. The water should be absorbed, with some starchy, saucy liquid left in the bottom of the pan. If there is too much liquid remaining, uncover and cook it off for a minute or two, stirring often.

4. Taste, add salt and pepper as needed, and serve.

Allergy Variation Tip: If you are not allergic to dairy, you may add grated Parmesan cheese as desired before serving. Or you may wish to add a shredded dairy-free cheese.

Per Serving: Calories: 447; Total fat: 15g; Sodium: 47mg; Carbohydrates: 73g; Fiber: 11g; Protein: 7g

Mushroom Soup

Serves 4
Prep time: 5 minutes
Cook time: 25 minutes

- 5 or Fewer Ingredients
- 30 Minutes or Less
- One-Pot
- Vegan

¼ cup extra-virgin olive oil

⅔ cup chopped shallots

2 tablespoons chopped garlic

6 cups coarsely chopped mushrooms

4 cups peeled and chopped yellow potato

8 cups vegetable broth

Salt

Freshly ground black pepper

This mushroom soup is so creamy you might think there's dairy in it, but it's absolutely dairy-free. Potatoes add a filling starchy component without overshadowing the depth of the fungi. Some mushrooms offer a wealth of vitamin D, which is especially important if you are prone to sitting in front of a screen all day as opposed to soaking up the sun outside.

1. In a large pot over medium-low heat, warm the olive oil. Add the shallots and garlic and cook them for about 2 minutes, until they are translucent and fragrant.

2. Add the mushrooms, increase the heat to medium, and cook for 5 minutes, until browned. Add the potatoes and broth, mixing to combine. Increase the heat to high and bring to a boil. Cook for about 15 minutes, or until the potatoes are fully cooked through and the broth is reduced by about 20 percent.

3. Puree the soup using an immersion blender or transfer the soup to a heat-safe standing blender and blend until smooth.

4. Taste and add salt and pepper as needed, then serve.

Substitution Tip: If you are not vegetarian or vegan, try chicken broth or stock in place of vegetable broth. Chicken stock is a great source of collagen, and the flavor pairs beautifully with mushrooms.

Per Serving: Calories: 215; Total fat: 6g; Sodium: 211mg; Carbohydrates: 35g; Fiber: 5g; Protein: 7g

Pumpkin Risotto

Serves 4
Prep time: 5 minutes
Cook time: 25 minutes

- ■ 5 or Fewer Ingredients
- ■ 30 Minutes or Less
- ■ One-Pot
- ■ Vegan

⅓ cup extra-virgin olive oil
3 garlic cloves, sliced
1½ teaspoons fresh or dried thyme
1½ cups arborio rice
4 cups vegetable broth
1⅓ cups pure pumpkin puree

Risotto may feel difficult and fancy, but it's just a simple rice dish. What makes risotto unique is the starchy nature of the arborio rice used to make it. Unlike other varieties of rice where you may rinse the starch away several times before cooking, the slow process of drawing the starch out with the addition of hot liquid is what gives risotto its characteristic creamy consistency.

1. In a medium saucepan over medium-low heat, warm the olive oil. Add the garlic and thyme and cook for about 1 minute, until fragrant.

2. Add the rice and stir to combine. Add the broth, ½ cup at a time, stirring well and waiting for the liquid to absorb after each addition. Cook the rice until tender, about 20 minutes total.

3. Add the pumpkin puree, stirring well. Cook for another 2 minutes, stirring often to prevent sticking. Serve warm.

Ingredient Tip: When buying pumpkin puree, be sure to pick one that is 100 percent pure pumpkin (not a pie filling or seasoned pumpkin mix). You can make your own pumpkin puree from roasted pumpkin flesh if you wish. Quarter a pie pumpkin, seed and stem it, and place each piece cut-side down on a rimmed baking sheet. Add ¼ cup of water, roasting at 375°F for 40 minutes. Peel off the skin and puree the pumpkin flesh until smooth.

Per Serving: Calories: 446; Total fat: 18g; Sodium: 10mg; Carbohydrates: 64g; Fiber: 5g; Protein: 6g

Bright and Fresh Summer Squash Soup

Serves 4
Prep time: 10 minutes
Cook time: 20 minutes

- 30 Minutes or Less
- One-Pot
- Vegan

2 tablespoons
  extra-virgin olive oil
⅓ cup finely chopped
  onion
Salt
Freshly ground black
  pepper
3 cups chopped
  zucchini and/or
  summer squash
2 cups peeled and
  chopped sweet
  potato
1 cup drained and
  rinsed canned white
  beans, Romano
  beans, or chopped
  green beans
1½ cups fresh parsley
4 cups vegetable broth
2 tablespoons freshly
  squeezed lemon juice

Sweet potato lovers, this one's for you. This summery soup is slightly sweet thanks to the natural sugars in sweet potato and zucchini. This soup is soft and light with velvety textures and bursting with color.

1. In a medium pot over medium heat, warm the olive oil. Add the onion and sweat for about 2 minutes, until translucent and fragrant. Season with salt and pepper.

2. Add the zucchini, sweet potato, beans, and parsley, stirring to combine. Cook, stirring often, for 2 to 3 minutes.

3. Add the broth and bring to a boil. Reduce the heat to low and simmer for 15 to 18 minutes, then season again with salt and pepper.

4. Stir in the lemon juice before serving.

Allergy Variation Tip: If you are not allergic to wheat or do not have celiac disease, add ½ cup dried soup pasta of your choosing and boil according to the instructions on the package.

Per Serving: Calories: 207; Total fat: 7g; Sodium: 98mg; Carbohydrates: 30g; Fiber: 7g; Protein: 7g

Sun-Dried Tomato and Red Bell Pepper Soup

Serves 4
Prep time: 5 minutes
Cook time: 20 minutes

- 5 or Fewer Ingredients
- 30 Minutes or Less
- One-Pot
- Vegan

¼ cup extra-virgin olive oil, plus more for serving

2 tablespoons coarsely chopped garlic

3 large bell peppers, cut into large pieces

⅓ cup sun-dried tomatoes (about 10 sun-dried tomatoes)

2 cups water

1 cup tomato puree

Salt

Black pepper

1 cup loosely packed fresh basil leaves

This thick, rich soup is an explosion of vibrant color and flavor. Sun-dried tomatoes are like a savory candy that complements the tartness of bell peppers and basil leaves very well. This soup is balanced, energizing, and full of vitamins. To add more fiber to this recipe, add a can of drained and rinsed white kidney beans or Romano beans after blending the soup and heat through for 5 minutes.

1. In a medium pot over medium heat, heat the olive oil and garlic for about 1 minute, until fragrant.

2. Add the bell pepper and cook for about 2 minutes, then add the sun-dried tomatoes, water, and tomato puree, stirring to combine. Season with salt and pepper.

3. Bring to a boil and cook, uncovered, for 15 to 18 minutes, until reduced in volume by about 20 percent.

4. Add the fresh basil and, using an immersion blender or heat-safe standing blender, puree until the soup is smooth and creamy with green flecks throughout.

5. Serve garnished with a drizzle of olive oil and a pinch of salt and pepper. Add a couple of fresh basil leaves if you have any remaining.

Flavor Boost: Toast your favorite allergy-free bread, or grab a sleeve of your favorite allergy-free crackers, and get dunking.

Per Serving: Calories: 202; Total fat: 14g; Sodium: 75mg; Carbohydrates: 17g; Fiber: 5g; Protein: 3g

Green Bean and Potato Salad with Mint

Serves 4
Prep time: 10 minutes
Cook time: 15 minutes

- **5 or Fewer Ingredients**
- **30 Minutes or Less**
- **Vegan**

5 cups mini yellow
 potatoes
Salt
3 cups halved green
 beans
1½ cups loosely packed
 mint leaves
½ cup extra-virgin
 olive oil
¼ cup freshly squeezed
 lemon juice
Freshly ground black
 pepper

A new take on a classic Italian recipe, this quick salad has incredible texture and unexpected flavors. The profile of mint changes significantly once heated and wilted, compared to when eaten cold. This recipe is fabulous when served hot, but it also holds up well in the refrigerator, making it a great make-ahead lunch idea.

1. In a large pot, completely cover the potatoes with water. Season with salt. Boil for 10 to 12 minutes, or until the potatoes are just fork-tender. Add the beans and continue cooking for another 2 minutes.

2. Use a colander to drain the potatoes and beans, then return to the pot and add the mint, olive oil, and lemon juice. Season with salt and pepper. Toss well, allowing the starch from the potatoes to mingle with the olive oil and lemon and coat the beans and serve.

Flavor Boost: Sprinkle red pepper flakes or hot chili oil on top as desired.

Per Serving: Calories: 426; Total fat: 27g; Sodium: 65mg; Carbohydrates: 42g; Fiber: 9g; Protein: 6g

Quick Rapini with Seeds and Red Pepper Flakes

Serves 4
Prep time: 5 minutes
Cook time: 10 minutes

- 5 or Fewer Ingredients
- 30 Minutes or Less
- One-Pot
- Vegan

¼ cup extra-virgin olive oil

2 tablespoons finely chopped garlic

2 bunches rapini, chopped

Salt

Freshly ground black pepper

⅔ cup shelled pumpkin seeds (salted or unsalted) or 3 tablespoons flaxseed

Red pepper flakes

¼ cup freshly squeezed lemon juice

The assertive bitter taste of rapini, also known as broccoli rabe, is sure to awaken your palate. Classically combined with garlic and red pepper flakes, this version incorporates protein-rich seeds to round out the dish and make it suitable for a quick one-pan meal. Serve it with a side of your favorite allergy-free toast if you desire a starchy component.

1. In a large skillet over medium heat, warm the olive oil and garlic for 1 to 2 minutes, or until fragrant. Do not brown the garlic.

2. Add the rapini, stirring to combine. Cook for 6 to 8 minutes, tossing every few minutes to ensure the greens cook evenly, until the rapini is tender but not mushy. Add salt and pepper as needed.

3. Add the seeds and red pepper flakes to taste, stirring to combine.

4. Take off the heat, then add the lemon juice right before serving.

Ingredient Tip: Select a brand of pumpkin seeds that has an allergy-free indication on the package, as seeds are often cross-contaminated with allergens such as nuts or peanuts during processing.

Per Serving: Calories: 260; Total fat: 24g; Sodium: 117mg; Carbohydrates: 8g; Fiber: 4g; Protein: 9g

Creamy Tuscan Sun-Dried
Tomato Chicken, page 68

CHAPTER 5

Poultry

Creamy Tuscan Sun-Dried Tomato Chicken

Serves 4
Prep time: 5 minutes
Cook time: 30 minutes

- 5 or Fewer Ingredients
- One-Pot

¼ cup extra-virgin olive oil

4 boneless, skinless chicken breasts

4 cups sliced mushrooms

3 cups spinach or kale

⅓ cup sun-dried tomatoes (about 10 sun-dried tomatoes)

2 cups gluten-free oat milk

This one-pan chicken dinner has protein, veggies, savory sun-dried tomatoes, and a creamy dairy-free sauce. The sauce keeps the chicken moist and tender, and the mushrooms and sun-dried tomatoes add a generous amount of flavor and texture to the dish.

1. In a large pan over high heat, warm the olive oil. Add the chicken and sear on both sides for about 3 minutes each until golden brown. Turn the heat down to medium-high and add the mushrooms and cook for about 3 minutes.

2. Add the spinach and sun-dried tomatoes, stirring to combine. Pour in the oat milk, cover, and reduce the heat to medium-low. Simmer for about 20 minutes, or until the chicken is tender its internal temperature reaches 165°F.

3. Portion into bowls and serve.

Ingredient Tip: In this recipe I recommend using dehydrated sun-dried tomatoes. They are typically found in the spice or condiment aisle, as opposed to the sun-dried tomatoes that are packed in oil and found in the olive aisle. Dehydrated sun-dried tomatoes tend to be less expensive and contain fewer ingredients than those jarred with oil and spices. To save time, you can buy sliced fresh mushrooms.

Per Serving: Calories: 308; Total fat: 18g; Sodium: 92mg; Carbohydrates: 7g; Fiber: 2g; Protein: 30g

Chicken and Carrot Pan Bake

Serves 4
Prep time: 5 minutes
Cook time: 25 minutes

- 5 or Fewer
  Ingredients
- 30 Minutes or Less
- One-Pot

4 cups sliced carrots
**4 boneless, skinless
  chicken breasts**
**¼ cup extra-virgin
  olive oil**
2 teaspoons paprika
**¼ cup balsamic
  vinegar**
Salt
**Freshly ground black
  pepper**

Simple ingredients come together for a stress-free weeknight meal. The carrots become lovely and crispy while the chicken stays tender and juicy. Make extra of this dish so that you can use the left-over chicken in soup the following day.

1. Preheat the oven to 400°F and line a baking sheet with parchment paper.

2. Spread out the carrots on the prepared baking sheet, then nestle the chicken in. Drizzle the olive oil evenly over the chicken and carrots, making sure the entire chicken breast is coated.

3. Sprinkle the paprika on top of the chicken, then drizzle the vinegar over the carrots. Season everything with salt and pepper.

4. Bake, uncovered, for 25 minutes, or until the chicken is tender and its internal temperature reaches 165°F.

Flavor Boost: Brush the chicken breasts with your favorite allergy-free hot sauce after drizzling with oil, then sprinkle the paprika on top of the layer of hot sauce.

Per Serving: Calories: 325; Total fat: 17g; Sodium: 144mg; Carbohydrates: 16g; Fiber: 4g; Protein: 27g

Tomato and Black Olive
Stewed Chicken

Serves 4
Prep time: 5 minutes
Cook time: 25 minutes

- 5 or Fewer Ingredients
- 30 Minutes or Less
- One-Pot

¼ cup extra-virgin olive oil

½ cup sliced onion

8 boneless, skinless chicken thighs

3 cups crushed tomatoes

1½ cups pitted black olives

Large handful fresh basil leaves, coarsely torn

This recipe is a balance of acidity and healthy fats. Dark meat chicken and olives meld together with acidic tomatoes and fresh and spicy basil. This meal can be eaten alone or with your choice of starch: allergy-free spaghetti, rice, or toast.

1. In a large pan over medium heat, warm the olive oil. Add the onion and cook until translucent, about 3 minutes.

2. Add the chicken, tomatoes, and olives, cover, and simmer for 20 minutes, or until the chicken's internal temperature reaches 165°F. Shred the chicken in the pan using two forks, then mix it up with the olives and sauce.

3. Add the fresh basil, mix well, and serve.

Substitution Tip: To make this recipe vegetarian, replace the chicken with 4 cups of cauliflower florets and reduce the simmering time to 15 minutes.

Per Serving: Calories: 448; Total fat: 26g; Sodium: 871mg; Carbohydrates: 18g; Fiber: 5g; Protein: 37g

Chicken Cacciatore

Serves 4
Prep time: 15 minutes
Cook time: 25 minutes

- 5 or Fewer Ingredients
- One-Pot

¼ cup extra-virgin olive oil
1½ cups chopped onion
1½ cups chopped celery
1½ cups chopped carrots
3 cups crushed tomatoes
4 chicken breasts, cut into ½-inch-wide pieces

Chicken cacciatore typically takes quite a while to simmer, but this version speeds things up. The sauce is loaded with chunks of veggies that not only contribute dimension but also nutrition to the velvety sauce.

1. In a large pot over medium heat, warm the olive oil. Add the onion, celery, and carrots and cook, stirring often, for 3 to 5 minutes, until the onion is translucent.

2. Add the tomatoes and chicken and toss well. Reduce the heat to medium-low, cover, and simmer for 15 minutes, or until the chicken is tender and no longer pink.

3. Uncover, increase the heat to medium-high, and let the sauce reduce for about 5 minutes, until thickened. Serve.

Ingredient Tip: Pulpy crushed tomatoes are also called "passata" or "polpa" in Italian and typically come in a glass jar, though you may also find them in a can. Passata refers to a fully pureed tomato product, whereas polpa refers to very finely chopped tomatoes packed in tomato juice. They may also be called crushed tomatoes. Feel free to use any of these options in this recipe.

Flavor Boost: Add ¼ to ½ cup of finely chopped fresh parsley at the very end.

Per Serving: Calories: 413; Total fat: 25g; Sodium: 470mg; Carbohydrates: 22g; Fiber: 6g; Protein: 28g

Grilled Chicken and Zucchini Skewers

Serves 4 to 6
Prep time: 15 minutes
Cook time: 10 minutes

- ■ 5 or Fewer
  Ingredients
- ■ 30 Minutes or Less

4 boneless, skinless
  chicken breasts
4 zucchini
1 cup extra-virgin olive
  oil
½ cup apple cider
  vinegar or freshly
  squeezed lemon juice
2 tablespoons dried
  oregano
1 teaspoon salt
1 teaspoon freshly
  ground black pepper

Chicken and veggie skewers are a friendly recipe for any beginner grill master. The juicy zucchini bookends the chicken so that it does not dry out on the grill. And the marinade is herby, light, and very quick to whip up.

1. Soak wooden skewers in water for 10 minutes to prevent them from burning on the grill. You can use metal skewers instead if you have them. Prepare a grill for high heat or set a grill pan over high heat.

2. Meanwhile, cut the chicken into 1-inch cubes and the zucchini into ½-inch half-rounds.

3. In a large bowl, whisk together the olive oil, vinegar, oregano, salt, and pepper. Add the chicken and zucchini to the marinade and mix it around so everything is well coated.

4. Thread the chicken and zucchini alternately onto the skewers, leaving at least 1½ inches of empty space on each end of the skewer.

5. Place the skewers on the grill and cook for about 10 minutes, or until the chicken is tender and no longer pink. Within the first few minutes of grilling, brush some of the remaining marinade onto the skewers to help them caramelize and stay moist.

6. Remove from the grill and serve.

Flavor Boost: Add 1 tablespoon of grated or finely chopped garlic to the marinade.

Per Serving: Calories: 293; Total fat: 17g; Sodium: 213mg; Carbohydrates: 7g; Fiber: 2g; Protein: 28g

Baked Sweet Chicken Wings

Serves 4
Prep time: 15 minutes
Cook time: 30 minutes

- ■ 5 or Fewer
  Ingredients
- ■ Worth the Wait

About 2 pounds split
  chicken wings
1 tablespoon
  extra-virgin olive oil
¼ cup maple syrup
¼ cup packed brown
  sugar
1 tablespoon finely
  chopped garlic
1 tablespoon
  cornstarch or tapioca
  starch
½ teaspoon salt
¼ teaspoon freshly
  ground black pepper

Frozen chicken wings are a quick go-to protein for many, but it can be difficult to find a safe brand if you have food allergies, such as dairy, wheat, or soy. Making your own fresh wings couldn't be easier. The rack allows the air to circulate around the wings evenly and prevents the chicken from becoming too wet.

1. Preheat the oven to 420°F. Line a baking sheet with parchment paper, then place a baking rack on top of the parchment.

2. Line the wings up along the rack and brush or drizzle the olive oil on top, then bake for 20 minutes.

3. While the wings are baking, in a small bowl, whisk together the maple syrup, brown sugar, garlic, cornstarch, salt, and pepper.

4. Remove the tray of wings from the oven and brush on the sauce. Alternatively, you can toss the wings with the sauce in a bowl. Return the wings to the oven and bake for another 5 to 8 minutes, or until the wings are golden brown.

5. Broil for about 2 minutes to get a crispier outer crust. Keep a close eye on the wings while broiling as they can quickly burn. Serve.

Allergy Variation Tip: If you are not allergic to soy, whisk 2 tablespoons of soy sauce into the sauce before basting onto the wings.

Per Serving: Calories: 656; Total fat: 44g; Sodium: 298mg; Carbohydrates: 29g; Fiber: 0g; Protein: 40g

Chicken and Mushroom Skillet with Basmati Rice

Serves 4
Prep time: 10 minutes
Cook time: 20 minutes

- ■ **5 or Fewer Ingredients**
- ■ **30 Minutes or Less**
- ■ **One-Pot**

¼ cup extra-virgin olive oil
2 boneless, skinless chicken breasts sliced into ¼-inch strips
4 garlic cloves, coarsely chopped
3 cups sliced cremini or button mushrooms
Salt
Freshly ground black pepper
1 cup basmati rice
2½ cups water
1 cup finely chopped fresh dill

Three simple ingredients—chicken, mushrooms, and rice—are complemented by a flourish of flavor and color from an abundance of fresh dill. This dish is inspired by the combination of dill and basmati rice often found in Middle Eastern cultures. One small herb can take your chicken and rice to a whole new level, and since we eat with our eyes first, that vibrant green color is sure to whet your palate. And we can't forget about mushrooms, an excellent source of vitamin D.

1. In a large pan over high heat, warm the olive oil. Add the chicken, garlic, and mushrooms and cook for about 5 minutes, until everything is lightly golden brown. The chicken will not yet be cooked through. Season with salt and pepper.

2. Turn the heat down to medium-low and add the rice, stirring to combine. Pour in the water and make sure everything is submerged. Cover and simmer for 15 minutes, or until the water is absorbed and the rice is cooked through.

3. Fold in the chopped dill, then serve.

Flavor Boost: Replace the water with an equal amount of chicken broth or stock.

Per Serving: Calories: 374; Total fat: 15g; Sodium: 34mg; Carbohydrates: 41g; Fiber: 1g; Protein: 18g

Chicken Soup with Dried Seaweed

Serves 4
Prep time: 5 minutes
Cook time: 20 minutes

- 5 or Fewer
  Ingredients
- 30 Minutes or Less
- One-Pot

1 tablespoon canola or
avocado oil
1 tablespoon sliced
garlic
1½ cups chopped
cooked chicken (white
or dark meat)
4 cups chicken broth or
stock
½ teaspoon freshly
ground black pepper
12 ounces rice noodles
or rice pasta
Salt
2 nori sheets (dried
seaweed), cut or
ripped into small
strips

This soup was inspired by a fabulous Korean dish
called miyeok guk (also called Korean seaweed
and beef soup), which is mainly composed of beef,
seaweed, and garlic. However, in this recipe I have
paired those delicious flavors with leftover roasted
or baked chicken.

1. In a medium pot over medium-high heat,
   warm the oil. Add the garlic and cook for about
   2 minutes, until browned. Immediately reduce
   the heat to low and add the chicken, broth, and
   pepper. Simmer for 15 minutes.

2. Add the rice noodles and cook until tender
   according to package instructions. Taste and add
   salt as needed.

3. Spoon the soup into bowls, then add the shredded seaweed on top and serve.

Allergy Variation Tip: If soy sauce and sesame oil are
safe for you, then add as desired at the end, before
adding the dried seaweed.

Per Serving: Calories 535; Total fat: 21g; Sodium: 222mg;
Carbohydrates: 68g; Fiber: 1g; Protein: 14g

Grilled Chicken with Olive Tapenade

Serves 4
Prep time: 10 minutes
Cook time: 10 minutes

- 5 or Fewer Ingredients
- 30 Minutes or Less

½ cup extra-virgin olive oil, divided
½ teaspoon freshly ground black pepper, divided
4 teaspoons dried oregano, divided
¼ cup freshly squeezed lemon juice, divided
2 garlic cloves, coarsely chopped, divided
Salt
8 boneless, skinless chicken thighs
1 (6-ounce) can pitted black olives

You might want to put this olive tapenade on everything. (You have been warned.) The intense and briny taste of olive tapenade, paired with its creamy texture, is a perfect match for simple grilled chicken.

1. In a large bowl, make a marinade by whisking together ¼ cup of olive oil, ¼ teaspoon of pepper, 2 teaspoons of oregano, 2 tablespoons of lemon juice, and 1 garlic clove. Season with salt.

2. Add the chicken to the marinade and mix it around to coat well. Let sit for 5 minutes.

3. Meanwhile, prepare the olive tapenade. In a standard or mini food processor, combine the remaining ¼ cup of olive oil, ¼ teaspoon of pepper, 2 teaspoons of oregano, 2 tablespoons of lemon juice, 1 garlic clove, and the olives. Pulse until smooth. Taste and add salt as needed.

4. Prepare a grill for high heat or set a grill pan over high heat.

5. Grill the chicken thighs for about 10 minutes, flipping halfway through, or until their internal temperature reaches 165°F. Serve with a good dollop of tapenade on top of each thigh.

Flavor Boost: Add 1 tablespoon of drained capers to the olive tapenade before blending it up for an extra briny zing.

Per Serving: Calories: 324; Total fat: 19g; Sodium: 689mg; Carbohydrates: 3g; Fiber: 2g; Protein: 34g

Saucy Lemon and Black Pepper Chicken Skillet with Noodles

Serves 4
Prep time: 15 minutes
Cook time: 30 minutes

- 5 or Fewer Ingredients
- One-Pot
- Worth the Wait

¼ cup extra-virgin olive oil, plus more for serving

4 boneless, skinless chicken breasts, cut into ¼-inch dice

⅓ cup freshly squeezed lemon juice

3 teaspoons freshly ground black pepper

Salt

3½ cups chicken stock or vegetable broth

12 ounces allergy-free spaghetti or spaghettini

2 cups finely chopped fresh curly or flat-leaf parsley

Per Serving: Calories: 567; Total fat: 18g; Sodium: 114mg; Carbohydrates: 67g; Fiber: 8g; Protein: 38g

Don't let the simple name of this recipe mislead you—this dish is silky and satisfying. Cooking the noodles in the pan juices and stock means that each noodle absorbs all of that delicious essence and aroma. The starch from the noodles thickens the stock that remains in the bottom of the pan, turning it into a luscious sauce that melds the chicken and noodles together.

1. In a large pan over medium-high heat, warm the olive oil. Add the chicken and cook, stirring often, for about 5 minutes. Add the lemon juice and pepper and season with salt, stirring to combine.

2. Add the stock and bring to a boil. Cover, reduce the heat to medium-low, and simmer for a total of 25 minutes. Toward the end of cooking, add the pasta and cook until tender according to package instructions. For example, if the pasta takes 10 minutes, add it after the mixture has been boiling for 15 minutes. Cover while the pasta cooks, stirring every few minutes to prevent it from sticking together or from sticking to the bottom of the pan. After the pasta cooks, the leftover liquid will form a sauce.

3. Right before serving, add the parsley and toss well. Drizzle a little bit more olive oil on top and season with salt and pepper as needed.

Ingredient Tip: A long noodle, such as spaghetti or spaghettini, works best in this recipe to soak up all of the brothy sauce and intertwine with the abundance of fresh parsley added at the end. A brown rice pasta works well.

Rich Chicken and Kale Skillet

Serves 4
Prep time: 15 minutes
Cook time: 30 minutes

- ■ 5 or Fewer Ingredients
- ■ One-Pot
- ■ Worth the Wait

¼ cup extra-virgin olive oil

1 cup sliced onion

Salt

Freshly ground black pepper

2 boneless, skinless chicken breasts or 4 boneless, skinless chicken thighs

3 cups torn kale leaves

1 (15.5-ounce) can white kidney beans, drained and well rinsed

1 cup chicken or vegetable broth

Extend chicken breast meat with a can of luscious, fiber- and protein-rich white kidney beans, which also creates a smooth sauce when mixed with the kale and onions. This hearty one-pot stew feels perfectly comforting in the colder months.

---

1. In a large nonstick pan over medium-high heat, warm the olive oil. Add the onion and cook, stirring often, for 5 to 7 minutes, or until starting to brown. Season with salt and pepper.

2. Add the chicken, kale, beans, and broth. Season with salt and pepper. Reduce the heat to medium-low, cover, and simmer for about 20 minutes, or until the chicken is tender and no longer pink.

3. Using the back of a fork, mash up about half of the beans, then shred the chicken using two forks. Stir to combine the mixture so that the creamy beans are coating everything evenly.

4. Taste, add salt and pepper as needed, and serve.

Allergy Variation Tip: If you are not allergic to dairy, add some freshly grated hard cheese, such as Parmesan, before serving. If you do have a dairy allergy, season with dairy-free nutritional yeast before serving.

Per Serving: Calories: 289; Total fat: 15g; Sodium: 32mg; Carbohydrates: 19g; Fiber: 5g; Protein: 19g

Fusilli with Chicken and Broccoli

Serves 4
Prep time: 10 minutes
Cook time: 20 minutes

- ■ 5 or Fewer Ingredients
- ■ 30 Minutes or Less
- ■ One-Pot

¼ cup extra-virgin olive oil, divided

1 tablespoon sliced garlic

2 boneless, skinless chicken breasts, cut into ½-inch cubes

4 cups 1-inch broccoli florets

2½ cups chicken or vegetable broth or stock

8 ounces allergy-free fusilli

Salt

Freshly ground black pepper

This dish features three very accessible and simple ingredients: chicken, broccoli, and noodles. While they may be simple, this recipe creates a nicely balanced meal with a cruciferous veggie, lean protein, and carbs. It also packs well for lunch.

1. In a large nonstick pan over high heat, warm the olive oil. Add the garlic and chicken and cook for about 5 minutes, until starting to brown. The chicken should be cooked about halfway through.

2. Add the broccoli and broth, stirring to combine. Cook, covered, for 15 minutes total, adding the pasta when needed according to package instructions. For example, if the pasta needs 10 minutes, add it after 5 minutes of cooking. Make sure all the pasta is submerged.

3. Uncover when the pasta is cooked, turn the heat to high, and let any residual liquid simmer off.

4. Taste and add salt and pepper as needed, then serve.

Flavor Boost: Fold in 1 cup of finely chopped parsley at the very end, as well as 2 tablespoons of lemon juice.

Per Serving: Calories: 419; Total fat: 16g; Sodium: 61mg; Carbohydrates: 49g; Fiber: 7g; Protein: 24g

Leftover Roasted Chicken Soup with Cilantro and Tomato

Serves 4
Prep time: 10 minutes
Cook time: 20 minutes

- 30 Minutes or Less
- One-Pot

2 tablespoons
  extra-virgin olive oil
½ cup finely chopped
  onion
2 cups chopped cooked
  chicken (white or dark
  meat, skin removed)
1½ cups coarsely
  chopped fresh cilantro
1 cup large-diced
  tomatoes or halved
  cherry tomatoes
¼ teaspoon freshly
  ground black pepper
Salt
4 cups chicken stock or
  water
8 ounces allergy-free
  short-cut pasta
Juice of 1 lemon

What a tasty way to use up leftover roast chicken. This is no boring sandwich. This soup marries the lovely flavors of tomato, chicken broth, and cilantro to create a complex and layered profile. It is absolute comfort food. Fresh cilantro contains important nutrients such as folate and vitamins, and the tomatoes are a great source of antioxidants.

1. In a medium pot over medium heat, warm the olive oil. Add the onion and cook for about 3 minutes, until translucent. Add the chicken, cilantro, and tomatoes, stirring to combine. Add the pepper and season with salt.

2. Add the stock and bring to a simmer. Cook for about 5 minutes, then add the pasta and cook until tender according to package instructions.

3. Just before serving, stir the lemon juice into the soup.

Flavor Boost: Add 1 teaspoon of ground turmeric after cooking the onion.

Per Serving: Calories: 384; Total fat: 11g; Sodium: 85mg; Carbohydrates: 47g; Fiber: 6g; Protein: 28g

Pork Chops in Cherry White Wine Sauce, page 86

Meat

Quinoa Cobb Skillet

Serves 4
Prep time: 5 minutes
Cook time: 30 minutes

- ■ 5 or Fewer Ingredients
- ■ One-Pot

12 ounces bacon
1½ cups corn kernels
Salt
Freshly ground black pepper
1½ cups quinoa
2½ cups water
5 ounces fresh spinach
2 avocados, peeled, pitted, and sliced

This one-pan skillet meal is inspired by a Cobb salad, featuring greens, bacon, avocado, and corn. It will work well for any meal of the day and packs well for lunches. While there is no creamy, dairy-based dressing as in a typical Cobb salad, the avocado acts as a healthy fat and adds creaminess to the skillet. Quinoa cooks quickly and adds an earthy flavor to the recipe.

1. Place the bacon in a large cold skillet. Set it over medium heat and cook, turning when the bacon browns and releases on one side, for about 10 minutes, or until crispy. Transfer it to a cutting board and chop it into small pieces. Return it to the skillet.

2. Add the corn and cook for 1 minute. Season with salt and pepper.

3. Add the quinoa and mix well. Pour in the water and ensure the quinoa is fully submerged. Reduce the heat to low, cover, and simmer for 15 minutes, or until the quinoa is fully cooked and the water is absorbed. Fold in the spinach and allow it to wilt.

4. Place the sliced avocado on top, then serve.

Flavor Boost: Squeeze the juice of 1 or 2 limes over the skillet right before serving.

Ingredient Tip: Fresh corn sliced off the cob works best; however, you can use an allergy-free frozen corn or drained canned corn.

Per Serving: Calories: 901; Total fat: 63g; Sodium: 715mg; Carbohydrates: 61g; Fiber: 13g; Protein: 27g

Sweet Chile and Lime Grilled Pork

Serves 4
Prep time: 15 minutes
Cook time: 15 minutes

- 5 or Fewer Ingredients
- 30 Minutes or Less

½ cup extra-virgin olive oil
¼ cup freshly squeezed lime juice
¼ cup honey
Salt
Freshly ground black pepper
2 teaspoons red pepper flakes
1 to 1¼ pounds boneless rib end cut or center loin cut pork, cut into 4 slices
1 head Boston lettuce

The nice balance of sweetness, bitterness, and spice of the marinade in this recipe results in juicy and delicious grilled pork and a well-dressed simple salad.

1. In a small bowl, whisk together the olive oil, lime, and honey. Season with salt and black pepper. Transfer half of this dressing to a separate bowl and reserve for the greens later.

2. Add the red pepper flakes to the remaining dressing and mix well. Pour the dressing into a dish and add the pork. Coat both sides of the pork in the dressing, and let it sit for 10 minutes to marinate.

3. While the meat is marinating, prepare a grill for high heat or set a grill pan over high heat.

4. Place the pork on the grill and sear on each side for 5 to 7 minutes, or until its internal temperature reaches at least 145°F. Brush the excess dressing from the dish onto the pork chops while they are cooking.

5. Meanwhile, toss the greens in the reserved dressing (not the one you used for the pork) and serve alongside the pork.

Substitution Tip: To make this recipe vegetarian, replace the pork with four large portabella mushrooms. Let them soak up the marinade before grilling so that they become nice and caramelized when they hit the heat of the grill.

Per Serving: Calories: 452; Total fat: 31g; Sodium: 141mg; Carbohydrates: 20g; Fiber: 1g; Protein: 28g

Pork Chops in Cherry White Wine Sauce

Serves 4
Prep time: 5 minutes
Cook time: 25 minutes

- ■ **5 or Fewer Ingredients**
- ■ **30 Minutes or Less**

1 tablespoon extra-virgin olive oil
1 to 1¼ pounds boneless rib end cut or center loin cut pork, cut into 4 slices
Salt
Freshly ground black pepper
¼ cup finely chopped shallot
1 cup white wine
1 cup pitted black cherries
2 rosemary sprigs

This elegant dish features golden-brown caramelized pork in a fruity and acidic white wine jus. Fresh rosemary ties the flavors together. Cherries are a great source of choline, a nutrient that aids in proper brain function.

1. In a large nonstick skillet over high heat, warm the olive oil. Add the pork and sear on each side for 3 to 5 minutes, or until golden brown with crispy bits. Season with salt and pepper.

2. Add the shallot and let it soak up the browned juices for 1 minute.

3. Turn the heat to medium-low and add the wine to deglaze the skillet, scraping up any brown bits. Add the cherries and rosemary, cover, and simmer for 15 minutes. Taste and add salt and pepper as needed.

4. Serve the pork with the jus spooned on top.

Ingredient Tip: Wine can contain all kinds of allergens and does not require ingredients labeling, like food does. There is no way to know what is in the wine you are drinking unless you reach out to the company or they voluntarily label ingredients. Egg white, fish, and dairy (casein, whey, or skim milk) are all commonly used in wine filtration and preservation processes. I recommend sticking with a brand of wine that you trust and one that is willing to share allergen information with you.

Per Serving: Calories: 282; Total fat: 18g; Sodium: 95mg; Carbohydrates: 6g; Fiber: 1g; Protein: 24g

Fried Pork and Hash Browns with Scallions

Serves 4
Prep time: 10 minutes
Cook time: 25 minutes

■ One-Pot

1 tablespoon
extra-virgin olive oil
3 cups yellow potatoes,
cut into ½-inch cubes
⅔ pound boneless rib
end cut or center
loin cut pork, cut into
½-inch cubes
Salt
Freshly ground black
pepper
3 tablespoons maple
syrup
2 tablespoons apple
cider vinegar
1 tablespoon tomato
paste
2 teaspoons paprika
1 cup finely chopped
scallions, both green
and white parts

This is a one-pan skillet meal with a homemade seasoning mix, reminiscent of barbecue sauce, with tomato paste, vinegar, and paprika. Scallions add a zesty bite at the end and bring color to this simple and inexpensive weeknight dish.

1. In a large nonstick pan over high heat, warm the olive oil. Add the potatoes to one-half of the pan and the pork to the other. Season with salt and pepper. Cook for 5 minutes, then reduce the heat to medium-low, cover, and cook for 15 minutes, until the potatoes are tender and the pork's internal temperature reaches at least 145°F. There should be lots of crispy bits on the bottom of the pan.

2. Add the maple syrup, vinegar, tomato paste, and paprika and stir to combine. Season with salt and pepper. Increase the heat to medium and cook, stirring often, for 2 to 3 minutes, until the flavors meld.

3. Sprinkle the scallions on top, then serve.

Allergen Variation Tip: If you are not allergic to eggs, fry two eggs and toss them on top before serving.

Per Serving: Calories: 298; Total fat: 10g; Sodium: 91mg; Carbohydrates: 33g; Fiber: 4g; Protein: 19g

Maple-Glazed Pork Chops with Greens

Serves 4
Prep time: 5 minutes
Cook time: 20 minutes

- 5 or Fewer
  Ingredients
- 30 Minutes or Less
- One-Pot

2 tablespoons
   extra-virgin olive oil
4 (8-ounce) pork chops
Salt
Freshly ground black
   pepper
⅓ cup apple cider
   vinegar
¼ cup maple syrup
Pinch red pepper
   flakes
8 cups loosely packed
   spinach, chard, or
   kale

Can't find a wine that works for your allergies? The good news is that you can create a savory jus with vinegar in the same way that you can with wine—by deglazing a skillet filled with tasty caramelized bits. Maple syrup balances the acidity of the vinegar and the subtle spice of the red pepper flakes.

1. In a large skillet over high heat, warm the olive oil.

2. Add the pork and cook on each side for 5 to 7 minutes, until both sides are browned and caramelized and the pork's internal temperature reaches at least 145°F. If the pork chops look pale, the skillet is not hot enough. Season the chops well with salt and pepper.

3. Reduce the heat to medium, then add the vinegar to deglaze the skillet, scraping up any browned bits. Add the maple syrup and red pepper flakes and swirl the skillet around to combine all the juices.

4. Stack the pork chops on one side of the skillet and add the greens to the other side. Toss them around in the juices and cook for about 3 minutes, or until just wilted.

5. Taste and add salt, pepper, and red pepper flakes as needed, then serve.

Flavor Boost: Add 2 to 3 finely chopped garlic cloves to the skillet before deglazing with vinegar.

Per Serving: Calories: 485; Total fat: 23g; Sodium: 199mg; Carbohydrates: 17g; Fiber: 2g; Protein: 50g

Pork Medallions with Chives and Rice

Serves 4
Prep time: 15 minutes
Cook time: 25 minutes

- **5 or Fewer Ingredients**
- **30 Minutes or Less**
- **One-Pot**

3 tablespoons
  extra-virgin olive oil
12 ounces pork loin, cut
  into ½-inch cubes
1 tablespoon ground or
  grated fresh ginger
Salt
Freshly ground black
  pepper
¾ cup basmati rice
1½ cups water
1 cup chopped chives
2 tablespoons apple
  cider vinegar

Rice and pork get an exciting upgrade with ginger, chives, and vinegar. Vinegar adds a complex umami flavor while chives and ginger add a fresh zing. This is a simple and satisfying comfort food meal.

1. In a large nonstick pan over medium-high heat, warm the olive oil. Add the pork and cook, stirring often, for 5 minutes, until nicely browned. Use a splatter guard, if you have one, to prevent the stove from becoming a hot mess.

2. Add the ginger, then season with salt and pepper, stirring to combine.

3. Add the rice and toast for 1 minute. Pour in the water and ensure all the rice is submerged. Reduce the heat to low, cover, and cook for 15 minutes, until the rice is tender.

4. Uncover, add the chives and vinegar, and season with salt and pepper. Toss everything together well, then serve.

Allergy Variation Tip: If you are not allergic to soy or gluten, drizzle the finished skillet with soy sauce.

Per Serving: Calories: 372; Total fat: 17g; Sodium: 80mg; Carbohydrates: 30g; Fiber: 1g; Protein: 21g

Lamb Kebabs

Serves 4
Prep time: 15 minutes
Cook time: 10 minutes

- ■ **5 or Fewer Ingredients**
- ■ **30 Minutes or Less**

---

2 pounds boneless lamb shoulder, cut into 1-inch cubes

1 pineapple, cored and cut into 1-inch cubes

15 to 20 pearl onions, peeled

¼ cup extra-virgin olive oil

Salt

Freshly ground black pepper

¼ cup julienned fresh mint leaves

Pineapple, which is rich in vitamin C and antioxidants, adds juicy sweetness to these lamb kebabs, and they are well balanced by savory grilled onion and the earthy aroma of the lamb itself. As the grill heats the pineapple and onions, the juices coat the lamb chunks and keep them moist throughout the cooking process and also infuses them with flavor. Lamb is rich in two very important minerals, zinc and iron, which many people are often deficient in.

1. Prepare a grill for high heat or set a grill pan over high heat. Soak 8 to 10 wooden skewers in water for 10 minutes. Soaking will prevent them from burning on the grill.

2. Thread the pieces of lamb, pineapple, and pearl onions onto the prepared skewers in an alternating pattern. (You may have pieces of pineapple leftover.)

3. Brush the finished skewers lightly with the olive oil. Season with salt and pepper.

4. Place the skewers on the grill and cook for 3 to 5 minutes on each side, or until the lamb has reached the desired doneness. Do not overcrowd the grill.

5. Plate the skewers on a platter and sprinkle the mint leaves over them while still hot, then serve with a sauce of your choice.

Ingredient Tip: Use a fresh ripe golden pineapple for best results. Canned pineapple has added sugar and lacks the texture and consistency of the fresh fruit.

Per Serving: Calories: 874; Total fat: 65g; Sodium: 343mg; Carbohydrates: 36g; Fiber: 4g; Protein: 39g

Rosemary-Garlic Beef Skewers

Serves 4
Prep time: 15 minutes
Cook time: 10 minutes

- 5 or Fewer Ingredients
- 30 Minutes or Less

2 pounds beef sirloin, cut into 1-inch cubes
2 bell peppers, cut into 1-inch pieces
1 red onion, cut into ½-inch pieces
¼ cup extra-virgin olive oil
4 rosemary sprigs, leaves removed and finely chopped
1 tablespoon finely chopped garlic
Salt
Freshly ground black pepper

Rosemary and garlic are a perfect pairing, and here they saturate beef and veggies with deep, earthy flavor. The beauty of kebabs is that you can cook the meat and veggies in one go. Serve with your favorite starch and a tossed salad, and you have a complete meal.

1. Heat a grill to high heat or set a grill pan over high heat. Soak 8 to 10 wooden skewers in water for about 10 minutes. Soaking will prevent them from burning on the grill.

2. Thread the beef, bell peppers, and onion onto the prepared skewers in an alternating pattern. Leave at least 1 inch of empty skewer on each end.

3. In a small bowl, whisk together the olive oil, rosemary, and garlic. Spoon this mixture generously onto the skewers, ensuring that every nook and cranny of the beef and vegetables has been evenly coated. Season with salt and pepper.

4. Place the skewers on the grill and cook for 3 to 5 minutes on each side, or until the beef has reached the desired doneness.

5. Plate the skewers on a platter and serve.

Ingredient Tip: Avoid using precut stewing beef for this recipe as it will not tenderize on the grill. Instead opt for sirloin, which has an ideal ratio of fat to meat for grilling. Fat is flavor and keeps the meat moist on the grill. You can use tenderloin if you want something a little fancier.

Per Serving: Calories: 521; Total fat: 32g; Sodium: 124mg; Carbohydrates: 7g; Fiber: 2g; Protein: 48g

Flank Steak with Chimichurri

Serves 4
Prep time: 10 minutes
Cook time: 10 minutes

■ 30 Minutes or Less

1¾ pounds flank steak

1 tablespoon
   extra-virgin olive oil,
   plus ¾ cup

½ teaspoon freshly
   ground black pepper,
   plus more as needed

½ teaspoon salt, plus
   more as needed

2 cups coarsely
   chopped flat-leaf
   parsley (about 1 large
   bunch)

1 tablespoon dried
   oregano

1 large shallot

2 garlic cloves, peeled
   and left whole

¼ cup apple cider or
   red wine vinegar

Red pepper flakes

Parsley is a powerhouse herb that is packed with nutrition, texture, and flavor. In this recipe, it is the star of the show as the main herb in chimichurri, a bright green sauce that is spooned on top of the tender grilled flank steak.

1. Prepare a grill for high heat or set a grill pan over high heat.

2. Pat the steak dry with paper towels, then brush on 1 tablespoon of olive oil and season with salt and pepper.

3. Place the steak on the grill and sear for 3 to 5 minutes on each side, or until it has reached the desired doneness. Transfer to a cutting board and let it rest before thinly slicing it against the grain of the meat.

4. Meanwhile, make the chimichurri by combining the remaining ¾ cup of olive oil, ½ teaspoon of pepper, ½ teaspoon of salt, the parsley, oregano, shallot, garlic, vinegar, and red pepper flakes, to taste, in a food processor or mini food processor. Pulse until smooth.

5. Arrange the sliced meat on a platter and spoon the chimichurri generously on top. Serve a bowl of extra chimichurri on the side for those who want more.

Allergy Variation Tip: If you are not allergic to fish, this recipe can easily be made pescatarian. Chimichurri goes well with grilled fish such as salmon or branzino. Grill over charcoal for best results.

Per Serving: Calories: 415; Total fat: 26g; Sodium: 258mg; Carbohydrates: 2g; Fiber: 0g; Protein: 42g

Meatballs with Tomato Sauce and Zoodles

Serves 4
Prep time: 20 minutes
Cook time: 25 minutes

- ■ **5 or Fewer Ingredients**
- ■ **Worth the Wait**

1 pound extra-lean ground beef

1 tablespoon finely chopped garlic, plus 1 teaspoon

1 teaspoon salt, plus more as needed

⅓ cup gluten-free oat flour

2 tablespoons extra-virgin olive oil

1 (27-ounce) can whole plum tomatoes

Freshly ground black pepper

3 cups spiralized zucchini

Gluten-free oat flour is the secret ingredient in this meatball recipe. Traditional meatballs can be made with any variety of common allergens, such as egg, bread crumbs, and Parmesan cheese. Oat flour acts as the binder in this version and contributes the "bready" aroma without any gluten. It also absorbs and holds on to liquid, keeping the inside of the meatballs moist and tender.

1. In a medium bowl, combine the beef, 1 tablespoon of garlic, 1 teaspoon of salt, and the oat flour, mixing well to combine.

2. Using your hands, roll the meat mixture into 20 mini meatballs. They do not have to look perfect.

3. In a large skillet over high heat, warm the olive oil. Add the remaining 1 teaspoon of garlic and the meatballs. Fry on one side for 2 to 3 minutes, until browned. To prevent the meatballs from sticking, shake the skillet every so often to loosen them. Don't try to flip them with tongs or a spatula, as it will tear the meat.

4. Add the tomatoes to the skillet, crushing them with your hands as you go. (Alternatively, you can mash them with a fork.) Season with salt and pepper. Bring the tomatoes to a simmer, reduce the heat to medium, and cover. Cook for 15 minutes, then uncover and simmer for 5 minutes to allow the sauce to reduce.

5. Add the zoodles and toss everything together, or portion the zoodles onto plates and spoon the sauce and meatballs over top to serve.

Flavor Boost: Stir a handful of torn fresh basil leaves into the sauce before serving.

Ingredient Tip: San Marzano tomatoes are regarded as one of the most flavorful varieties of plum tomatoes, and among the best for making sauce. If you see a can of whole San Marzano tomatoes, give it a try. You'll notice a difference in both taste and texture.

Per Serving: Calories: 293; Total fat: 14g; Sodium: 685mg; Carbohydrates: 16g; Fiber: 5g; Protein: 28g

Personal-Size Meat Loaf

Serves 4
Prep time: 10 minutes
Cook time: 20 minutes

- 5 or Fewer
  Ingredients
- 30 Minutes or Less

1 pound extra-lean
  ground beef
1 teaspoon salt
½ teaspoon freshly
  ground black pepper
1 tablespoon dried
  oregano
1 tablespoon tomato
  paste, plus ½ cup
3 tablespoons brown
  sugar
¼ cup apple cider
  vinegar

The comforting aroma and taste of meat loaf without the long baking time. These personal-size meat loaves are coated in a quick ketchup-like sauce. This is a great recipe idea for kids who are learning to get involved in the kitchen, as they can assist with mixing the sauce and shaping the cute little loaves.

1. Preheat the oven to 375°F and line a baking sheet with parchment paper.

2. In a medium bowl, mix the beef, salt, pepper, oregano, and 1 tablespoon of tomato paste. Divide the mixture into 8 equal pieces and form each one into a mini meat loaf shape. Place them on the prepared baking sheet, spaced about 1 inch apart.

3. In the same bowl you used for the meat, whisk together the remaining ½ cup of tomato paste, the brown sugar, and vinegar. Spoon the sauce evenly over the meat loaves, using it all.

4. Bake for 10 minutes, then turn the oven up to 410°F and bake for 5 minutes more, or until the meat loaves' internal temperature reaches 160°F.

5. Turn on the broiler and broil the loaves for 2 to 3 minutes, until the tops are brown, keeping a close eye to ensure the sauce does not burn.

6. Portion out 2 loaves per person and serve right away.

Allergen Variation Tip: If you are not allergic to fish or legumes, add Worcestershire sauce to the tomato paste mixture, as desired, before spooning onto the meat loaves.

Per Serving: Calories: 220; Total fat: 6g; Sodium: 680mg; Carbohydrates: 17g; Fiber: 2g; Protein: 26g

Cilantro Beef Burgers

Serves 4
Prep time: 10 minutes
Cook time: 10 minutes

■ **30 Minutes or Less**

---

1 pound lean ground
    beef
½ cup finely chopped
    fresh cilantro
2 tablespoons finely
    chopped garlic
½ teaspoon salt
¼ teaspoon freshly
    ground black pepper
2 teaspoons paprika
Boston lettuce leaves,
    for serving
1 avocado, peeled,
    pitted, and sliced

Cilantro adds a pop of unexpected brightness and freshness to otherwise common beef burgers. Garlic adds a punch of flavor and is thought to be beneficial to the immune system.

1. In a medium bowl, combine the beef, cilantro, garlic, salt, pepper, and paprika.

2. Divide the meat mixture into 4 equal pieces and form into thin burger patties. A thinner patty will fry better if cooking on the stovetop.

3. Warm a large nonstick skillet over medium-high heat. Place the burgers in the skillet and cook for about 5 minutes on each side, or until the desired doneness is reached. (Alternatively, try cooking these on the grill.)

4. Serve in a Boston lettuce leaf with slices of avocado on top.

Allergy Variation Tip: If you are not allergic to gluten, serve the burgers and avocado slices on your favorite wheat buns.

Per Serving: Calories: 243; Total fat: 13g; Sodium: 373mg; Carbohydrates: 7g; Fiber: 4g; Protein: 26g

One-Pot Bolognese

Serves 4
Prep time: 15 minutes
Cook time: 30 minutes

- 5 or Fewer Ingredients
- One-Pot
- Worth the Wait

1 pound extra-lean ground beef
1½ cups chopped carrots
1½ cups chopped celery
2 cups crushed tomatoes
12 ounces allergy-free spaghetti
2½ cups water
Salt

Traditional Bolognese sauce features meat soaked in milk and often in a sauce containing dairy and little tomato. While this version of the dish is different from the traditional recipe, it is influenced by American-style spaghetti Bolognese and still serves up a meaty tomato sauce intertwined with pasta that any pasta lover would enjoy.

1. In a large skillet over medium-high heat, cook the beef, stirring and breaking it into small pieces, for about 6 minutes, until browned.

2. Drain off any excess fat, then add the carrots and celery and cook for about 10 minutes, until tender.

3. Add the tomatoes and mix well. Then add the pasta and water and season with salt, mixing to coat the noodles well. Reduce the heat to medium, cover, and cook for 5 minutes. Uncover and stir to ensure the noodles do not stick together, then cover again and cook for another 5 to 6 minutes, or until the noodles are tender. The water should be absorbed, and a light tomato sauce should remain in the skillet.

4. Divide onto plates and serve.

Flavor Boost: Replace the water with an equal amount of chicken stock.

Per Serving: Calories: 509; Total fat: 7g; Sodium: 409mg; Carbohydrates: 78g; Fiber: 11g; Protein: 39g

Zesty Fried Beef and Rice

Serves 4
Prep time: 10 minutes
Cook time: 25 minutes

- 5 or Fewer Ingredients
- One-Pot

2 tablespoons extra-virgin olive oil

1 pound beef stir-fry strips

Salt

Freshly ground black pepper

1 cup thinly sliced onion (about ½ large onion)

3 cups sliced red bell peppers (about 2 bell peppers)

1 cup brown or white basmati rice

2 cups water

1½ cups allergy-free salsa

All the flavor and beauty of a stuffed pepper without the time commitment. This skillet is a casual meal that is bursting with zesty flavors and colorful veggies. Premade salsa is a real time-saver, especially on a hectic weeknight.

1. In a large nonstick skillet over high heat, warm the olive oil. Season the beef with salt and pepper. Add it and the onion to the skillet and stir-fry for about 5 minutes, then add the peppers and mix well. Stir-fry for another 2 minutes, until the peppers are browned.

2. Turn the heat down to medium-low and add the rice, mixing well. Add the water and ensure that all the rice is submerged. Cover and cook for 15 minutes, until the rice is tender and the liquid is absorbed.

3. Add the salsa and toss well. Turn the heat up to medium and cook, stirring, for 2 to 3 minutes, or until the salsa is heated through.

4. Portion onto plates and serve.

Flavor Boost: Sprinkle on ¼ cup of chopped fresh chives before serving.

Allergen Variation Tip: If you are not allergic to dairy, add your favorite shredded cheese as desired at the end.

Per Serving: Calories: 437; Total fat: 13g; Sodium: 543mg; Carbohydrates: 49g; Fiber: 5g; Protein: 31g

Salty Chocolate Chip Cookies, page 105

Desserts

Drizzled Fruit Skewers

Serves 6
Prep time: 20 minutes, plus 1 hour to chill
Cook time: 5 minutes

- ■ **5 or Fewer Ingredients**
- ■ **Vegan**
- ■ **Worth the Wait**

½ pint fresh strawberries, stemmed
½ pint fresh raspberries
1 pint fresh blueberries
½ pint fresh blackberries
1½ cups allergy-free dark chocolate, chopped
Toppings of choice, such as allergy-free sprinkles, mini chocolate chips, or flaky sea salt (optional)

Per Serving: Calories: 297; Total fat: 18g; Sodium: 9mg; Carbohydrates: 30g; Fiber: 9g; Protein: 4g

This is a simple dessert that you can make and enjoy or make ahead of time. There's no need to overcomplicate delicious berries that are bursting with flavor just as they are. And in the summer months when turning on the oven feels daunting, it's a great idea to have this quick and cold recipe up your sleeve.

1. Wash all the berries well and gently and thoroughly pat them dry with a paper towel. If they are wet, the chocolate will not stick. Line a baking sheet with parchment paper.

2. Thread the berries onto 8 to 10 skewers in whatever pattern you prefer. Be sure to leave room on the end as a handle. Place the skewers on the prepared baking sheet.

3. Place the chocolate in a microwave-safe bowl. Melt the chocolate in the microwave on low power in 30-second intervals, stirring in between each heating. Transfer the chocolate to a pastry bag or a zip-top bag and snip the corner off.

4. Drizzle the melted chocolate over the fruit skewers.

5. Leave the skewers as they are, or add the toppings of your choice. Roll them in the toppings or sprinkle the toppings on, depending on how much you want on each skewer.

6. Chill the tray of skewers in the refrigerator for 1 hour before serving.

Ingredient Tip: You can make this recipe with red and green grapes (seedless is preferable) instead of berries.

"Banana Bread" Nice Cream

Serves 4
Prep time: 10 minutes

- 5 or Fewer Ingredients
- 30 Minutes or Less
- One-Pot
- Vegan

5 bananas, peeled, sliced, and frozen

2 tablespoons maple syrup

1 teaspoon ground cinnamon, plus more for garnish

1 teaspoon pure vanilla extract

This dairy-free, ice cream–like dessert tastes just like a tasty slice of banana bread. Similar to a very thick smoothie, nice cream is a quick blender sorbet. Eat it immediately to enjoy its rich and creamy texture before it melts away.

1. Place the bananas in a food processor and pulse until they resemble gravel.

2. Add the maple syrup, cinnamon, and vanilla and pulse until smooth and creamy.

3. Spoon the nice cream into bowls and add a dash of ground cinnamon on top of each one before serving.

Substitution Tip: The maple syrup is optional in this recipe and can be adjusted to suit your sweetness preference. If you are not vegan, you may also replace it with honey.

Per Serving: Calories: 162; Total fat: 1g; Sodium: 3mg; Carbohydrates: 41g; Fiber: 4g; Protein: 2g

Citrus-Berry Nice Cream

Serves 4
Prep time: 10 minutes

- 5 or Fewer Ingredients
- 30 Minutes or Less
- One-Pot
- Vegan

4 bananas, peeled, sliced, and frozen
1 cup frozen blueberries
2 tablespoons freshly squeezed orange or lemon juice
1 tablespoon maple syrup
Fresh blueberries or orange segments, for garnish

A light and refreshing alternative to ice cream, nice cream is a thick and creamy frozen dessert made with bananas, frozen fruit, and other flavorings. Despite being a tasty dessert recipe, you can easily make this for breakfast instead of a smoothie. Just add your choice of seeds on top for protein.

1. Place the bananas in a food processor and pulse until they resemble gravel.

2. Add the blueberries, orange juice, and maple syrup and pulse until smooth and creamy.

3. Spoon the nice cream into bowls and garnish with fresh blueberries and/or orange segments for color.

Ingredient Tip: When fruit is in season and more abundant and affordably priced, you can freeze your own. Make sure you freeze it flat so that it doesn't become a big mound. Purchasing frozen fruit is a great alternative in the winter or if you do not have adequate access to fresh produce in your region.

Per Serving: Calories: 145; Total fat: 1g; Sodium: 2mg; Carbohydrates: 37g; Fiber: 4g; Protein: 2g

Salty Chocolate Chip Cookies

Makes 16 cookies
Prep time: 15 minutes
Cook time: 15 minutes

- 30 Minutes or Less
- Vegan

2 tablespoons chia
seeds
½ cup rice milk,
gluten-free oat milk,
or water
1 cup allergy-free
buttery spread
1 cup packed dark
brown sugar
¼ cup powdered sugar
1 teaspoon pure vanilla
extract
2 cups gluten-free
1-to-1 flour mix
1¼ teaspoons baking
soda
1½ teaspoons xanthan
gum
Pinch salt
½ cup allergy-free
chocolate chips
½ cup allergy-free
pretzel pieces

Per Serving: (1 cookie):
Calories: 237; Total fat: 8g;
Sodium: 164mg;
Carbohydrates: 38g;
Fiber: 2g; Protein: 2g

Food allergies are no reason to miss out on classic chocolate chip cookies, and these are taken up a notch with salty, crispy pretzel pieces. Chia seeds are an amazing egg substitute as they puff up and become gloopy, mimicking the texture of egg white. They bind the dough together and keep the inside moist and tender. These cookies are cakey and soft in the center with a crispy outer crust and crunchy bottom.

1. Preheat the oven to 375°F and line a large baking sheet with parchment paper.

2. In a small bowl, mix the chia seeds and rice milk, then let the mixture sit for 5 minutes, until the seeds are sticky and slimy.

3. Meanwhile, in a large bowl, beat together the buttery spread, brown sugar, powdered sugar, and vanilla until smooth. Add the prepared chia seeds and beat well.

4. Add half of the gluten-free flour, beating until just combined. Then add the remaining flour, baking soda, xanthan gum, and salt, beating until just combined.

5. Fold in the chocolate chips and pretzel pieces.

6. Divide the dough into 16 equal pieces and roll each one into a ball. Space them out 1 inch apart on the prepared baking sheet to allow them room to spread in the oven. Do not flatten the tops.

7. Bake for 10 minutes for softer cookies and 12 to 14 minutes for crunchy cookies. Let cool slightly, then serve.

Fruit and Cinnamon Oat Bake

Serves 6
Prep time: 15 minutes
Cook time: 25 minutes

- One-Pot
- Vegan

6 cups sliced fruit, such
   as apples, peaches,
   or pears
¾ cup gluten-free oats
¼ cup packed dark
   brown sugar
½ teaspoon pure
   vanilla extract
½ teaspoon ground
   cinnamon
Pinch salt
6 tablespoons
   allergy-free buttery
   spread
1 tablespoon
   granulated sugar
   (optional)

Fill your kitchen with the cozy scent of fruit pie without having to make a filling or roll out a crust. This oat bake is a simple and foolproof dessert that is ideal for anyone who prefers their treats less sweet.

1. Preheat the oven to 375°F.

2. In a 10-by-7-inch baking dish, combine the fruit, oats, brown sugar, vanilla, cinnamon, and salt. Mix well so that the fruit is evenly coated.

3. Cover the dish with aluminum foil and bake for 20 minutes. Remove the foil and add the buttery spread in pieces to the top of the mixture, dispersed somewhat evenly.

4. Bake, uncovered, for another 5 minutes, until the juice is bubbling. If you wish to caramelize the crust, sprinkle the granulated sugar on top and broil for 1 to 2 minutes, or until golden brown.

5. Remove from the oven, let cool slightly, and serve warm in small bowls.

Flavor Boost: Serve with a side of your favorite allergy-free ice cream.

Ingredient Tip: The type of fruit you use in this dessert will impact the final texture and taste. If using apples, opt for a soft cooking apple such as McIntosh. For pears, use a creamy, ripe pear such as Bosc. Use peaches when they are in season so that they are at their juiciest.

Per Serving: Calories: 199; Total fat: 6g; Sodium: 110mg; Carbohydrates: 34g; Fiber: 4g; Protein: 4g

Grilled Pineapple with Raspberry Sauce

Serves 6
Prep time: 20 minutes
Cook time: 10 minutes

- ■ **5 or Fewer Ingredients**
- ■ **30 Minutes or Less**
- ■ **Vegan**

1 pineapple, peeled, cored, and cut into 6 equal rounds
½ pint fresh raspberries
2 tablespoons maple syrup
1 tablespoon water

Ingredient Tip: A pre-peeled and cored fresh pineapple will work in this recipe; however, canned pineapple would not work well.

Per Serving: Calories: 103; Total fat: 0g; Sodium: 3mg; Carbohydrates: 27g; Fiber: 3g; Protein: 1g

This simple fruit dessert is both sweet and tart. Grilling the pineapple adds a toasty aroma while the inner flesh becomes super juicy and warm. The raspberry sauce adds life to the plate with a hit of color and vibrancy, and it makes the pineapple feel extra special. You can use this raspberry sauce on other desserts to add that little extra something.

1. Prepare a grill (preferably charcoal) for high heat or set a grill pan over high heat. Place the pineapple on the grill and cook for about 3 minutes on each side, until grill marks appear.

2. Meanwhile, in a small saucepan over medium heat, combine the raspberries, maple syrup, and water. Cook, mashing the raspberries with a fork on the bottom of the pan, for 5 to 7 minutes, until the fruit is broken down. Use an immersion blender to blend until smooth.

3. Strain the raspberry mixture through a fine-mesh sieve into a small bowl, being sure to scrape the pulp from the bottom of the sieve. The sauce should be liquid but not watery. Discard the seeds.

4. Arrange the grilled pineapple on a platter. Drizzle the raspberry sauce evenly across the slices. The pineapple shouldn't be swimming in sauce; it should just add a bit of tartness and color.

5. Serve warm.

Strawberry Custard

Serves 6
Prep time: 10 minutes, plus 30 minutes to chill (optional)
Cook time: 15 minutes

- 5 or Fewer Ingredients
- 30 Minutes or Less
- Vegetarian

¾ pint fresh strawberries, stemmed
2 cups gluten-free oat milk
⅓ cup cornstarch
2 tablespoons honey
1 tablespoon allergy-free buttery spread
Pinch salt

A creamy strawberry puree, lightly sweetened with honey, is combined with earthy oat milk to create a decadent pink custard. This dessert can be enjoyed immediately or can be made ahead of time and kept in the refrigerator until you are ready to serve.

1. In a mini food processor, puree the strawberries until smooth.

2. Transfer the puree to a large metal bowl, then add the oat milk, cornstarch, honey, buttery spread, and salt. Whisk to combine.

3. Prepare a double boiler by filling a small pot over medium heat with 1½ inches of water. Place the bowl on top of the pot, making sure it doesn't touch the water, and cook, stirring constantly, for about 15 minutes, or until the mixture thickens and coats the back of a spoon. (If you make a line with your finger on the back of a spoon, it should stay.)

4. Pour the mixture into individual serving cups while still warm, then tap them on the countertop to even out the tops.

5. Enjoy right away, or chill in the refrigerator for 20 to 30 minutes for a firm-set custard.

Allergy Variation Tip: An equal amount of rice milk can replace the oat milk, and if coconut is allergy safe for you, coconut milk is a suitable alternative as well.

Substitution Tip: For a vegan option, use maple syrup or agave syrup instead of honey.

Per Serving: Calories: 84; Total fat: 2g; Sodium: 55mg; Carbohydrates: 16g; Fiber: 1g; Protein: 2g

Strawberries with Homemade Chocolate Sauce

Serves 6
Prep time: 10 minutes

- ■ 5 or Fewer Ingredients
- ■ 30 Minutes or Less
- ■ One-Pot
- ■ Vegan

2 pounds fresh strawberries, stemmed and quartered, or berries of choice
½ cup maple syrup
⅓ cup pure cocoa powder
⅛ teaspoon sea salt
Fresh mint leaves, for garnish

What better way to finish off a weeknight dinner than with a very simple dessert that you can throw together on a whim? Chocolate sauce is incredibly simple to make at home with just three ingredients. Drizzle it over berries and top with fresh mint leaves for a delicate and homey treat.

1. Divide the berries equally among serving bowls or plates.

2. In a small bowl, whisk together the maple syrup, cocoa powder, and sea salt until well combined and smooth.

3. Drizzle the chocolate sauce over the bowls of berries. Garnish with mint leaves, then serve.

Ingredient Tip: Any berries will work in this recipe. Swap out the strawberries for fresh or frozen blueberries, raspberries, blackberries, cherries, golden berries, or even sliced bananas, depending on your taste preference.

Per Serving: Calories: 127; Total fat: 1g; Sodium: 57mg; Carbohydrates: 32g; Fiber: 4g; Protein: 2g

Lemon Bars

Makes 9 bars
Prep time: 20 minutes,
plus 1 hour to chill
Cook time: 10 minutes

- Vegetarian
- Worth the Wait

1 (5.3-ounce) package
  allergy-free crunchy
  vanilla cookies
1 tablespoon
  allergy-free buttery
  spread, plus ½ cup
1 cup freshly squeezed
  lemon juice
¾ cup cornstarch
½ cup honey
½ cup gluten-free oat
  milk
1 teaspoon pure vanilla
  extract
½ teaspoon ground
  turmeric
Pinch salt

Per Serving: (1 bar):
Calories: 268; Total fat:
12g; Sodium: 136mg;
Carbohydrates: 41g; Fiber:
1g; Protein: 2g

Lemon lovers, this recipe is for you. The lemon curd is tart and sweet with a silky-smooth texture. It is perfectly complemented by the quick and crispy crust made from allergy-free vanilla cookies.

1. Preheat the oven to 400°F and line an 8-inch square cake pan with parchment paper.

2. In a food processor or mini food processor, grind the cookies until they resemble sand. Add 1 tablespoon of buttery spread and pulse until the mixture resembles wet sand. Transfer it to the prepared pan and press it down firmly and evenly with a spoon. Bake for 5 minutes.

3. Prepare a double boiler by filling a small pot over medium heat with 1½ inches of water.

4. In a medium metal bowl, combine the remaining ½ cup of buttery spread, lemon juice, cornstarch, honey, oat milk, vanilla, turmeric, and salt.

5. Place the bowl on top of the pot, making sure it doesn't touch the water, and cook, stirring constantly, for 5 to 7 minutes, until the mixture melts and yellows. Keep stirring, scraping the bottom of the bowl to prevent any of the mixture from sticking, until it is thick, viscous, and coats the back of a spoon.

6. Pour the hot mixture onto the warm crust and smooth out the top. Let it rest for about 15 minutes, or until room temperature. Cover with plastic wrap and refrigerate for about 1 hour, or until the lemon curd has set.

7. Cut into 9 squares and serve.

Blueberry-Cinnamon Rice Pudding

Serves 6

Prep time: 20 minutes, plus 20 minutes to chill

Cook time: 10 minutes

- Worth the Wait
- Vegan

2 cups gluten-free oat milk or rice milk

⅓ cup tapioca starch

⅛ teaspoon salt

1 teaspoon pure vanilla extract

1 tablespoon maple syrup

½ teaspoon ground cinnamon

1 tablespoon allergy-free buttery spread

2 cups cooked arborio rice

½ pint blueberries

Although this dish is traditionally dotted with raisins, blueberries add a nice freshness and burst of flavor in this recipe variation. It's quite filling, so each modest serving goes a long way. Short-grain rice, particularly arborio rice, is starchy, which naturally thickens the dessert.

1. Prepare a double boiler by filling a small pot over medium heat with 1½ inches of water.

2. In a medium metal bowl, whisk together the oat milk, tapioca starch, salt, vanilla, maple syrup, cinnamon, and buttery spread.

3. Place the bowl on top of the pot, making sure it doesn't touch the water, and cook, stirring constantly, for about 5 minutes, until smooth and slightly thickened. Add the rice and stir well using a spatula. Cook for about 2 minutes, until thickened, then remove from the heat.

4. Spoon the pudding into serving cups, then add the blueberries on top while still hot.

5. Chill in the refrigerator for 15 to 20 minutes, or until set, then serve.

Allergy Variation Tip: If coconut is an allergy-safe option for you, use coconut milk and coconut oil in place of the rice milk and buttery spread for a smoother flavor.

Per Serving: Calories: 139; Total fat: 1g; Sodium: 88mg; Carbohydrates: 29g; Fiber: 2g; Protein: 2g

Avocado Ranch
Dressing, page 128

Staples

Rice Milk

Makes 7 cups
Prep time: 5 minutes

- **5 or Fewer Ingredients**
- **30 Minutes or Less**
- **One-Pot**
- **Vegan**

¾ cup cooked sushi rice, cooled
¾ cup cooked jasmine rice, cooled
5 to 5½ cups water
⅛ teaspoon salt

Rice milk made with cooked rice is silky and thicker in texture than store-bought rice milk. It makes a delicious addition to coffee, tea, or baked goods in place of dairy milk. The beauty of this rice milk recipe is that it does not have to be strained, making it faster and requiring less cleanup than other homemade milks. It's important to use cooled rice. The texture will be different (gloopy) if you use hot or warm rice.

1. In a blender, combine the sushi rice, jasmine rice, water, and salt. Blend for 1 minute, until smooth and creamy.

2. Transfer the rice milk to airtight bottles or jars and store in the refrigerator for up to 3 days.

Flavor Boost: Add 1½ teaspoons of pure vanilla extract and 2 tablespoons of maple syrup for vanilla rice milk. You can use brown rice in this recipe, but I recommend combining it with half white rice for a creamier texture, as brown rice can be more granular in nature.

Per Serving: (1 cup): Calories: 47; Total fat: 1g; Sodium: 41mg; Carbohydrates: 13g; Fiber: 0g; Protein: 0g

Oat Milk

Makes 3½ cups
Prep time: 15 minutes, plus 1 hour to soak

- 5 or Fewer Ingredients
- Vegan
- Worth the Wait

1 cup gluten-free oats
3 cups cold water, plus more for soaking
¼ teaspoon salt

Per Serving: (1 cup):
Calories: 45; Total fat: 2g; Sodium: 150mg; Carbohydrates: 6g; Fiber: 0g; Protein: 1g

While store-bought oat milk is an option, making your own at home is very easy and cost effective. It provides an opportunity to adjust the oat milk to your liking, controlling the sweetness, thickness, and flavor profile. Use this oat milk in savory dishes, smoothies, and baking, or add it to your morning coffee.

1. In a medium bowl, soak the oats in water for 30 minutes to 1 hour, then strain and discard that water.

2. Transfer the soaked oats to a blender. Add 3 cups of cold water and blend for 2 minutes, until well pulverized.

3. Line a large glass jar with a jelly bag (made of nylon or natural fiber), wrapping the elastic edge back up around the lip of the jar. If you do not have a jelly bag, you can use a linen cheesecloth. Pour the oat mixture into the jelly bag. Gently squeeze out the liquid.

4. Remove the jelly bag and rinse thoroughly, saving the oat pulp for baking or smoothies.

5. Pour the strained liquid back into the blender and add the salt. Blend for another 1 minute.

6. Transfer to airtight bottles or jars and store in the refrigerator for up to 3 days.

Flavor Boost: For vanilla oat milk, add 1 teaspoon of vanilla extract and 1 tablespoon of honey or maple syrup when you add the salt, then blend. For chocolate, add 1 teaspoon of vanilla extract, 2 tablespoons of maple syrup, and 2 tablespoons of pure cocoa powder when you add the salt.

Gluten-Free Bread Crumbs and Croutons

Makes 2 cups
Prep time: 5 minutes
Cook time: 10 minutes

- 5 or Fewer Ingredients
- 30 Minutes or Less
- Vegan

2 gluten-free bread slices of choice
1 garlic clove, halved
2 tablespoons extra-virgin olive oil
Salt
Freshly ground black pepper
2 teaspoons dried oregano

Store-bought bread crumbs often contain dairy, soy, and of course, wheat flour. Homemade bread crumbs are as simple as it gets. Keep them in an airtight container in the refrigerator for up to 3 days and use in meatballs, for breading chicken or other meats, or on top of baked dishes for a crispy crunch. Croutons can be tossed with green salads or tomato salads for a nice crunch and bit of carb to balance out a meal.

1. Preheat the oven to 420°F.

2. To make bread crumbs, place the bread on a baking sheet. Bake for 8 to 10 minutes, or until the bread is hard, crusty, and lightly golden brown. (Or use stale bread and bake a little less.) Let the bread cool enough to touch, then break it up into pieces and pulse it in a food processor until it resembles bread crumbs.

3. To make croutons, rub the bread with the flat side of the garlic. Cut the bread into cubes, then place on a baking sheet. Drizzle the olive oil on top, then sprinkle with salt, pepper, and oregano. Mix it up well so that everything is evenly coated. Bake for 8 to 10 minutes, or until crispy and golden brown.

Ingredient Tip: Rubbing the garlic on the bread as opposed to chopping it and mixing it up with the bread chunks allows it to be infused with garlic flavor while not risking the taste of burnt garlic bits.

Per Serving: (¼ cup): Calories: 71; Total fat: 4g; Sodium: 60mg; Carbohydrates: 6g; Fiber: 0g; Protein: 1g

Balsamic Vinaigrette

Makes 1 cup
Prep time: 5 minutes

- 5 or Fewer Ingredients
- 30 Minutes or Less
- One-Pot
- Vegetarian

½ cup extra-virgin olive oil
¼ cup balsamic vinegar
1 teaspoon dried oregano
1 garlic clove, minced
1 teaspoon honey
¼ teaspoon freshly ground black pepper
Salt

Every home cook needs to know how to make a delicious salad dressing. This recipe can be used on any type of green salad, quinoa, or chopped salads, or as a sauce on sandwiches.

In a small bowl, whisk together the olive oil, vinegar, oregano, garlic, honey, pepper, and salt. Taste and add more salt and pepper as needed. Store in an airtight container in the refrigerator for up to 3 days.

Ingredient Tip: Apple cider vinegar or red wine vinegar can be used instead of balsamic vinegar.

Flavor Boost: Add 1 tablespoon of Dijon mustard or grainy mustard and whisk well.

Per Serving: (2 tablespoons): Calories: 130; Total fat: 13g; Sodium: 22mg; Carbohydrates: 2g; Fiber: 0g; Protein: 0g

Pesto

Makes 1 cup
Prep time: 5 minutes

- ■ **5 or Fewer Ingredients**
- ■ **30 Minutes or Less**
- ■ **One-Pot**
- ■ **Vegan**

1½ cups fresh basil
¼ cup extra-virgin olive oil
¼ cup shelled pumpkin seeds (salted or unsalted)
2 tablespoons freshly squeezed lemon juice
2 garlic cloves, peeled and left whole
Salt
Freshly ground black pepper

Pesto is an Italian basil-based sauce that traditionally contains cheese and pine nuts and is ground with a mortar and pestle. In this version, the "nutty" flavor comes from earthy pumpkin seeds, and the mortar and pestle are replaced with a food processor. Toss pesto with hot pasta, use in cold pasta salads, spread on sandwiches, or dunk veggie sticks into it as a dip.

In a food processor or mini food processor, combine the basil, olive oil, pumpkin seeds, lemon juice, garlic, salt, and pepper and pulse until smooth. Taste and add salt and pepper as needed. Store in an airtight container in the refrigerator for up to 3 days.

Flavor Boost: Season with nutritional yeast for a cheesy flavor.

Per Serving: (1 tablespoon): Calories: 42; Total fat: 4g; Sodium: 15mg; Carbohydrates: 1g; Fiber: 0g; Protein: 1g

Raspberry Vinaigrette

Makes 1¼ cups
Prep time: 5 minutes

- ■ 5 or Fewer
  Ingredients
- ■ 30 Minutes or Less
- ■ One-Pot
- ■ Vegan

¾ cup fresh
  raspberries
½ cup extra-virgin
  olive oil
¼ cup freshly squeezed
  lemon juice
1 small shallot, peeled
1 teaspoon salt
¼ teaspoon freshly
  ground black pepper

Raspberry vinaigrette adds a pink pop of color to any leafy salad. The sweetness of the raspberry is balanced out by the fresh tartness of the lemon juice and the zestiness of the shallot. Toss this dressing with crisp Boston lettuce leaves or green salads that contain fruit, such as sliced pear or orange segments.

In a food processor or mini food processor, combine the raspberries, olive oil, lemon juice, shallot, salt, and pepper and pulse until smooth. Taste and add more salt and pepper as needed. Store in an airtight container in the refrigerator for up to 3 days.

Ingredient Tip: The flavor of shallot is a cross between onion and garlic, but with less sharpness, making it the perfect balancing factor in this mild dressing.

Per Serving: (2 tablespoons): Calories: 102; Total fat: 11g; Sodium: 233mg; Carbohydrates: 2g; Fiber: 1g; Protein: 0g

Poppy Seed Dressing

Makes 1⅔ cups
Prep time: 5 minutes

- ■ **5 or Fewer Ingredients**
- ■ **30 Minutes or Less**
- ■ **One-Pot**
- ■ **Vegetarian**

½ onion, coarsely chopped (about ¾ cup)

½ cup extra-virgin olive oil or canola oil

¼ cup apple cider vinegar

1 teaspoon salt

1 teaspoon honey

1 teaspoon poppy seeds

¼ teaspoon freshly ground black pepper

Did you know that onions can create a creamy texture when blended? This dressing is a great substitute for Caesar dressing or any other creamy salad dressing. The flavor is unexpectedly rich and tangy.

In a food processor or mini food processor, combine the onion, olive oil, vinegar, salt, honey, poppy seeds, and pepper and pulse until smooth. Taste and add more salt and pepper as needed. Store in an airtight container in the refrigerator for up to 3 days.

Ingredient Tip: Seeds are often produced in facilities where cross contamination with nuts or peanuts is possible, so opt for a brand that is free from common allergens as opposed to shopping in the bulk section of the store.

Per Serving: (2 tablespoons): Calories: 79; Total fat: 8g; Sodium: 180mg; Carbohydrates: 1g; Fiber: 0g; Protein: 0g

Barbecue Sauce

Makes 2½ cups
Prep time: 5 minutes
Cook time: 20 minutes

- 5 or Fewer
  Ingredients
- 30 Minutes or Less
- One-Pot
- Vegan

2 tablespoons
   extra-virgin olive oil
   or a neutral oil, such
   as avocado or canola
1 cup chopped onion
11 ounces tomato
   paste
¼ cup packed brown
   sugar
¼ cup apple cider
   vinegar
1 tablespoon paprika

Store-bought barbecue sauce can be made with any number of common allergens, from anchovies to soy. Fortunately, making your own barbecue sauce from scratch is simple and easy. This recipe is very basic and can be used for chicken wings, grilled chicken, pork chops, ribs, and more.

1. In a small pot over medium-low heat, warm the olive oil and cook the onion for about 15 minutes, or until the onion is very soft, translucent, and golden brown.

2. Add the tomato paste, brown sugar, vinegar, and paprika, mixing well. Reduce the heat to low and simmer for 5 minutes.

3. Using an immersion blender or a heat-safe blender, puree the sauce. Let cool, then store in an airtight container in the refrigerator for up to 3 days.

Allergy Variation Tip: If you are not allergic to fish, add 1 tablespoon of Worcestershire sauce when you add the tomato paste, paprika, sugar, and vinegar.

Ingredient Tip: Use a domestic tomato paste as opposed to an Italian concentrated tomato paste (the type that often comes in a metal tube). The domestic tomato pastes tend to be sweeter and milder in flavor, which lends itself better to this recipe.

Per Serving: (2 tablespoons): Calories: 40; Total fat: 1g; Sodium: 11mg; Carbohydrates: 7g; Fiber: 1g; Protein: 1g

Corn and Avocado Salsa

Makes 3½ cups
Prep time: 10 minutes
Cook time: 5 minutes

- **5 or Fewer Ingredients**
- **30 Minutes or Less**
- **Vegan**

---

1 cup fresh corn kernels

1½ cups chopped avocado

1 cup finely chopped fresh cilantro

2 tablespoons freshly squeezed lime juice

2 tablespoons extra-virgin olive oil

Salt

Freshly ground black pepper

A simple salsa with so many possibilities. Serve it on homemade tacos, dunk chips into it, serve with grilled chicken, or eat it as a quick little side salad. The bright and fresh flavors are ideal for summer.

---

1. In a small skillet over medium heat, sauté the corn for about 5 minutes, until cooked through. Let it cool while you prepare the other ingredients.

2. In a medium bowl, combine the avocado, cilantro, lime juice, olive oil, salt, and pepper, mixing well. Add the corn and toss together. Taste and add salt and pepper as needed.

3. Store in an airtight container in the refrigerator for up to 3 days.

Flavor Boost: Add red pepper flakes or chili powder as desired.

Per Serving: (¼ cup): Calories: 52; Total fat: 4g; Sodium: 34mg; Carbohydrates: 3g; Fiber: 1g; Protein: 1g

Chicken Broth

Makes 5½ cups
Prep time: 5 minutes
Cook time: 2 hours

- 5 or Fewer
  Ingredients
- Worth the Wait

1 pound chicken wings
  or thighs
8 cups water
2 celery stalks
1 large carrot
½ onion
2 teaspoons salt
2 teaspoons black
  peppercorns

Making your own chicken broth at home allows you to control exactly what goes into it, from salt content to spices to veggies. The measurements in this recipe do not have to be exact to create a delicious chicken broth, so if you have an extra onion or carrot you want to toss in, or perhaps a handful of fresh parsley, feel free to do so.

1. Preheat the oven to 400°F. Place a wire rack in a rimmed baking sheet.

2. Place the chicken pieces on the wire rack and roast for 30 minutes, until golden brown.

3. Transfer the chicken and the pan juices to a large pot over high heat. Add the water, celery, carrot, onion, salt, and peppercorns. Bring to a rolling boil, then reduce the heat to low and simmer for 1 hour, 30 minutes. (You may need to adjust the heat to maintain a simmer.)

4. Remove the broth from the heat. Strain the broth into jars and let cool, then lid and store in the refrigerator for up to 3 days or freeze for later use.

Ingredient Tip: For the chicken, use dark meat with the skin and bones intact, as that is where the flavor comes from.

Per Serving: (1 cup): Calories: 25; Total fat: 0g; Sodium: 775mg; Carbohydrates: 2g; Fiber: 1g; Protein: 2g

Vegetable Broth

Makes 5½ cups
Prep time: 5 minutes
Cook time: 1 hour
30 minutes

- One-Pot
- Vegan
- Worth the Wait

8 cups water
3 celery stalks
3 garlic cloves, peeled
   and left whole
2 large carrots
1 tomato
½ onion
Handful fresh parsley
2 teaspoons black
   peppercorns
1 teaspoon salt

A good vegetable broth has depth of flavor from a variety of veggies and flavorings. You can cook rice in vegetable broth or use it in any soup or in other savory dishes in place of water.

1. In a large pot over high heat, combine the water, celery, garlic, carrots, tomato, onion, parsley, peppercorns, and salt. Bring to a rolling boil, then reduce the heat to low and simmer for 1 hour, 30 minutes. (You may need to adjust the heat to maintain a simmer.)

2. Remove the broth from the heat. Strain the broth into jars and let cool, then lid and store in the refrigerator for up to 3 days or freeze for later use.

Ingredient Tip: Trim the vegetables and leave them whole in this recipe. There's no need for presentation as the vegetables get strained out before using the broth.

Per Serving (1 cup): Calories: 15; Total fat: 0g; Sodium: 330mg; Carbohydrates: 2g; Fiber: 0g; Protein: 0g

Avocado Ranch Dressing

Makes 1¾ cups
Prep time: 5 minutes

- 30 Minutes or Less
- One-Pot
- Vegan

1 garlic clove, peeled
  and left whole
1 cup avocado flesh
½ cup gluten-free oat
  milk
2 tablespoons canola
  or avocado oil
2 tablespoons apple
  cider vinegar
2 tablespoons
  chopped fresh chives
1 tablespoon minced
  fresh or dried dill
1 teaspoon paprika
½ teaspoon freshly
  ground black pepper
Salt

Ranch dressing gets an allergy-free makeover in this recipe with rich and silky avocado as the base. Oat milk makes the dressing light and fluffy, creating the ideal vehicle for all the flavorings and spices.

In a blender, combine the garlic, avocado, oat milk, canola oil, vinegar, chives, dill, paprika, salt, and pepper and blend until smooth. Taste and add more salt and pepper as needed. Store in an airtight container in the refrigerator for up to 3 days.

Flavor Boost: Add a few dashes of your favorite hot sauce or chili powder.

Per Serving: (2 tablespoons): Calories: 42; Total fat: 4g; Sodium: 12mg; Carbohydrates: 3g; Fiber: 1g; Protein: 0g

Measurement Conversions

VOLUME EQUIVALENTS	U.S. STANDARD	U.S. STANDARD (OUNCES)	METRIC (APPROXIMATE)
LIQUID	2 tablespoons	1 fl. oz.	30 mL
	¼ cup	2 fl. oz.	60 mL
	½ cup	4 fl. oz.	120 mL
	1 cup	8 fl. oz.	240 mL
	1½ cups	12 fl. oz.	355 mL
	2 cups or 1 pint	16 fl. oz.	475 mL
	4 cups or 1 quart	32 fl. oz.	1 L
	1 gallon	128 fl. oz.	4 L
DRY	⅛ teaspoon	–	0.5 mL
	¼ teaspoon	–	1 mL
	½ teaspoon	–	2 mL
	¾ teaspoon	–	4 mL
	1 teaspoon	–	5 mL
	1 tablespoon	–	15 mL
	¼ cup	–	59 mL
	⅓ cup	–	79 mL
	½ cup	–	118 mL
	⅔ cup	–	156 mL
	¾ cup	–	177 mL
	1 cup	–	235 mL
	2 cups or 1 pint	–	475 mL
	3 cups	–	700 mL
	4 cups or 1 quart	–	1 L
	½ gallon	–	2 L
	1 gallon	–	4 L

OVEN TEMPERATURES

FAHRENHEIT	CELSIUS (APPROXIMATE)
250°F	120°C
300°F	150°C
325°F	165°C
350°F	180°C
375°F	190°C
400°F	200°C
425°F	220°C
450°F	230°C

WEIGHT EQUIVALENTS

U.S. STANDARD	METRIC (APPROXIMATE)
½ ounce	15 g
1 ounce	30 g
2 ounces	60 g
4 ounces	115 g
8 ounces	225 g
12 ounces	340 g
16 ounces or 1 pound	455 g

Resources

There is a lot of conflicting information about life with food allergies on the internet. It's important to get your facts from credible sources, so here are a few trustworthy online resources about food allergies.

- *Allergic Living Magazine* | AllergicLiving.com

- FARE | FoodAllergy.org

- *Food Allergy Canada* | FoodAllergyCanada.ca

- Kids with Food Allergies | KidsWithFoodAllergies.org

- *The Itch Podcast* | ItchPodcast.com

- The Zestfull | TheZestfull.com

Books can be a classroom resource or a way to teach your child about the severity of their allergies and why they must carry epinephrine. They can also be a window into what diagnosis will look like at any age, what it means, and how life shapes up for teens and adults living with this disease. Here are my favorite books about life with food allergies.

- *Don't Kill the Birthday Girl* by Sandra Beasley

- *Living with Allergies: Practical Tips for All the Family* by Emma Amoscato

- *You, Me and Food Allergies* by Emma Amoscato

- *Zoey Has an Allergy* by Anisha Angella

References

Food Allergy Canada. "Allergens." Accessed December 23, 2021. FoodAllergy Canada.ca/allergies.

Food Allergy Canada. "Reading Food Labels." Accessed December 23, 2021. FoodAllergyCanada.ca/living-with-allergies/day-to-day-management /reading-food-labels.

Food and Agriculture Organization of the United Nations. "Food Groups and Sub-Groups." Accessed December 23, 2021. FAO.org/gift-individual-food -consumption/methodology/food-groups-and-sub-groups/en.

Hall, Rachel. "Lab-Grown Dairy Is the Future of Milk, Researchers Say." *Guardian*. July 31, 2021. TheGuardian.com/food/2021/jul/31/lab-grown -dairy-is-the-future-of-milk-researchers-say.

Kids with Food Allergies. "Wheat Allergy Avoidance List: Hidden Names for Wheat." Last updated March 2015. KidswithFoodAllergies.org/media /Wheat-Allergy-Avoidance-List-Hidden-Names.pdf.

U.S. Department of Agriculture. *Dietary Guidelines for Americans 2020–2025*. December 2020. DietaryGuidelines.gov/sites/default/files/2021-03 /Dietary_Guidelines_for_Americans-2020-2025.pdf.

Index

About the Author

Amanda Orlando has lived with food allergies her whole life. She is the blogger behind @EverydayAllergenFree, where she shares recipes and stories about her life with food allergies and eczema. In addition to this book, Amanda is the author of two other food allergy-friendly cookbooks, including *Everyone's Welcome: The Art of Living and Eating Allergen Free* and *Allergen-Free Desserts*. Her writing has appeared in *Allergic Living Magazine*, the *Globe and Mail*, and more. Amanda believes her stories are best told with optimism, honesty, and humor. She lives in Toronto, Canada.

CPSIA information can be obtained
at www.ICGtesting.com
Printed in the USA
LVHW070003230522
718847LV00003B/3